waking the buddha

waking
the buddha

how the most dynamic and empowering
buddhist movement in history is changing
our concept of religion

Clark Strand

MIDDLEWAY
PRESS

Published by Middleway Press
A division of the SGI-USA
606 Wilshire Blvd., Santa Monica, CA 90401

Cover and interior design by Gopa & Ted2, Inc.

10 9 8 7 6 5 4 3 2 1

ISBN 978-0-9779245-6-1

Library of Congress Cataloging-in-Publication Data

Strand, Clark, 1957- author.
  Waking the Buddha : how the most dynamic and empowering
Buddhist movement in history is changing our concept of
religion / Clark Strand.
    pages cm
  ISBN 978-0-9779245-6-1 (paperback)
  1. Soka Gakkai International 2. Buddhism—Social aspects.
I. Title.
  BQ8415.4.S87 2014
  294.3'928–dc23

                                                    2013049938

 Middleway Press is committed to preserving
ancient forest and natural resources. We are a
member of the Green Press Initiative—a nonprofit program dedicated to supporting book publishers in maximizing their use of
fiber, which is not sourced from ancient or endangered forests.
We have elected to print this title on Natures B19 Smooth Antique,
made with 30 percent post consumer waste. For more information
about the Green Press Initiative and the use of recycled paper in
book publishing, visit www.greenpressinitiative.org

contents

the spark
an idea ahead of its time

the foundation
the creation of the soka gakkai

the development
the discovery of modern buddhism

the completion
the spread of religious humanism

the future
a religion for the twenty-first century

the spark

an idea ahead of its time

a change in the life of
one individual

IN FEBRUARY OF 2003, just weeks before the U.S. invasion of Iraq, I came across a photograph of some Buddhist prayer beads made in a Tokyo prison during World War II. With limited resources to draw from, a prisoner of conscience had improvised them using the bottle caps from his daily milk ration.

I found the "beads" in the photograph strangely moving, even beautiful. Not that they were elegantly made. Far from it. The cardboard bottle caps were dark from handling and worn to the point of falling apart. Nevertheless, the photo inspired me to learn more about the imprisonment of Josei Toda—the man who had made them and then later became the president of the Nichiren Buddhist lay group the Soka Gakkai (Value Creation Society). A month later, I wrote a short article for an American Buddhist magazine that began with a series of questions:

> What goes through the mind of the person who chooses to go to jail rather than betray his

spiritual convictions, the person who, refusing
to be swept up in the militant patriotism that
precedes most wars, chooses loneliness and
isolation instead? It is hard enough to imagine
how such a person passes the days and weeks.
What of the hours and minutes? Isn't it con-
ceivable that the resolve of the heart might
collapse under the weight of even a single
moment?

The article went on to describe how Toda and his mentor, Tsunesaburo Makiguchi, had been arrested by the
government as "thought criminals" because of their
refusal to support the Japanese war machine. Makiguchi had died in prison, but Toda survived, renewing his
resolve day by day, bottle cap by bottle cap—a moment's
weight . . . added to another moment's weight . . . added
to another.

Sometime later, when a friend asked why I'd become
interested in the Soka Gakkai, I knew the answer right
away. Toda hadn't collapsed. He'd borne up under the
weight of countless moments when it would have been
easier to accept defeat.

One of the most striking things about the Soka Gakkai
from a Buddhist point of view is its emphasis on attaining victory in ordinary life—sometimes under *extra*ordinary circumstances, like the ones Toda had endured.

Soka Gakkai members chant the mantra-like title of the Lotus Sutra, Nam-myoho-renge-kyo, as a way of harnessing the universal life force inherent in their own bodies and minds. According to the teachings of Nichiren Buddhism, that mantra activates the basic, positive creative energy of the universe—a force that animates all sentient beings, driving them to grow and express their true nature eternally, from one lifetime to the next. By chanting Nam-myoho-renge-kyo and working for the happiness of others, Nichiren Buddhists seek to improve their current life condition and demonstrate "actual proof" of the Buddhist principle that all things are interconnected—that an inner change in the life of one individual can trigger outer changes in their community, their environment, and ultimately the world at large.

That principle of interconnectedness corresponds with what we know today about particle physics and planetary ecology, both of which support the view that all things are intimately interrelated and dependent upon one another—that nothing exists as separate and alone. Before Nichiren, however, that teaching was mostly theory, a topic for discussion between religious intellectuals or debate among cloistered monks and nuns. It didn't have much application outside of the sedate (some might say sleepy) world within temple or monastery walls. The idea that individuals could use it to awaken to the possibilities for change in everyday life, producing positive effects in their own lives and the lives of those around them, honoring their responsibilities to society and to the life of the planet itself—that had never been put to the test.

Nichiren changed all that. He staked his life on that theory, making it the basis of his teaching and standing alone against the corrupt military government of thirteenth-century Japan. Like Toda and Makiguchi seven centuries later, he believed that religion should serve the lives of individuals rather than merely functioning as a pawn of the state. And, also like Toda and Makiguchi, he ran afoul of the government and of the religious institutions that supported it. Twice attacked, twice exiled, and once sentenced to execution for his uncompromising views, Nichiren refused to back down from his belief that ordinary people could change their karma and attain enlightenment in this lifetime simply by chanting Nam-myoho-renge-kyo. It was a revolutionary vision of Buddhism that empowered lay people to take charge of their spiritual and material destiny, and he was widely condemned for it.

Today, you might call Nichiren Buddhism "an idea way ahead of its time." After Nichiren's death, the school of Buddhism he founded grew steadily but never became the dominant voice of Buddhism in Japan. When Toda left prison in 1945, it was just what it had been for centuries: a small sect with a big teaching that had never really come into its own. Were it not for his efforts, and those of his successor, Daisaku Ikeda, it is unlikely that anybody outside of Japan would ever have heard of it. As it is, the Soka Gakkai, the largest and most influential lay group in Buddhist history, has now spread the teachings of Nichiren Buddhism to some 192 countries around the globe. How and why that happened, and what it means for religion in the twenty-first century, is the subject of this book. It's the story of an idea whose time has come, and of the people who made it a reality.

the flame of reform

L IFE IS A STRUGGLE. That is one way of understanding the first noble truth of Buddhism: that life is suffering. Given that reality, it is no surprise that human beings the world over tend to experience their lives in terms of whether they are winning that struggle or not—in other words, in terms of gain and loss. And yet, these are seldom emphasized by religion. Marx called religion "the opiate of the masses." Granted, he judged religion mostly on the basis of its failures; nevertheless, it is fair to say that religions the world over have tended to prefer conformity over revolution, complacency over action. Religious teachings offer inspiration and consolation but rarely spark the fire of revolution. Societies prefer the elegant confinement of the candle on the altar over the open flame of reform.

Religions usually grow out of some revolutionary impulse initially—in the beginning they may attempt to address racial or ethnic discrimination or economic inequality. However, as time goes on they invariably choose stability over all else, even at the expense of

the ongoing spiritual evolution of humankind. Having
woken us up initially, they allow us to grow drowsy again,
sometimes for decades or centuries on end. That is probably why I felt drawn to the story of Toda's resistance to
the war. It was the wake-up call I had been expecting
from American Buddhism in the lead-up to the Iraq War,
a call that never actually arrived.

In retrospect, I'm not sure why I expected American
Buddhism to provide such a call. With the exception of
the Soka Gakkai International (SGI), all major schools
of Buddhism in America have their origins in the teachings of pre-modern traditions, the appeal of which rests
largely upon their antiquity. They are attractive to most
converts precisely because they do *not* engage modern
issues but provide some solace—in the form of ritual
or silent meditation—from the issues and problems of
modernity. This may account, in part, for the popularity
of the weekend or week-long retreat model so prevalent in American Buddhism, which provides a kind of
"spiritual vacation" from many aspects of modern culture—such as most forms of current communication,
including phone, e-mail, the Internet, and news bulle-
tins. It is ironic that American Buddhism won the bulk
of its initial converts during the countercultural years
of the 1960s only to become religiously complacent, if
not exactly conservative in the usual sense, as it grew in
subsequent decades.

Doubtless, some of this is due to the inevitable aging and "settling" of the baby boomer generation who first embraced Buddhism, but I can't help wondering if Buddhism didn't also provide us with an escape route from the social turbulence of that era, with its antiwar protests and civil rights marches. The natural rhythms of religious culture seem to involve a certain amount of waking and dozing, only to wake and doze again.

Several years ago, I wrote an article for *Tricycle: The Buddhist Review* pointing out that, by the year 2000, SGI-USA was the only school of Buddhism in the United States to have attracted a racially diverse membership, the other Buddhist groups being composed primarily of upper middle-class Americans of European descent. I suggested that the various other schools of American Buddhism might do well to ask themselves why, in a society as diverse as America's, their memberships were so monocultural. In a letter to the editor, one reader defended that monoculture as follows: "When one is meditating with eyes closed or gazing at the floor, all Buddhist centers seem to look pretty much alike." The author seemed quite comfortable with an eyes-wide-shut approach to Buddhism that allowed him to ignore issues of race and class. Thinking back, I have to ask myself if maybe he'd once been *very* aware of such issues—only he'd forgotten them. Buddhism had become a way of meditatively "tuning out" certain social realities and relaxing into the normalcy of a relatively privileged middle-class life. Ironically, his meditation practice had become a way of falling asleep.

Given this phenomenon, it is all the more ironic that the Soka Gakkai has often been criticized in America for its focus on such middle class values as economic success and security. The comment I most often hear when I speak of Nichiren Buddhism to other American Buddhists is "they're the ones who chant for stuff like cars and money, right?" Because such comments often come from these upper middle-class Buddhists of European decent who have rarely had to worry about money or cars, I've generally felt obliged to point out the hypocrisy of criticizing others for wanting the very things that they already have and therefore take for granted. Nowadays, however, that argument has lost much of its edge.

Today many Soka Gakkai members who joined the movement during the 1960s and '70s have attained the financial security they sought. Open the pages of the *World Tribune* (SGI-USA's weekly newspaper) and, true to the SGI tradition of reaching out to the disenfranchised and the destitute, you will find stories from those who have recently risen from adversity. But you will also find articles about U.S. congressmen, corporate executives, university professors, doctors, lawyers, artists, and an impressive number of successful small-business owners. Naturally, even those who have attained prosperity still struggle with health issues, relationships, and the countless other challenges of daily life, and as a lifelong path, Nichiren Buddhism helps them to overcome those obstacles to happiness as well. Nevertheless, apart from its racial makeup, which continues to be far more diverse than any other American Buddhist group, the gap between SGI members and devotees of predominantly white, upper middle-class Buddhist groups is gradually decreasing. Sadly, that hasn't affected the perception of Nichiren Buddhism as a kind of "prosperity church." It has, however, changed the way I respond to such misperceptions.

Today, when met with comments like "they chant for money," I answer that, while financial security is certainly an issue for some, we shouldn't let that distract us from the fact that SGI members also chant for the happiness of their friends and family, for human rights and human dignity, and for equal treatment of gays and women and minorities, or that they exert their influence and enthusiasm as a collective body to guarantee religious freedoms for *all* people—not just for Buddhists. To these I add that many also chant for an end to unprovoked military aggression such as the U.S. war with Iraq. In short, Nichiren Buddhists continue to chant for and take action on behalf of those very "lost values" of the 1960s and '70s that many American Buddhists, although they may also hold such values, do not see as imperatives of a Buddhist life. It is a forceful argument, but a good one, though it occasionally ruffles some feathers. A few of my Buddhist friends have pointed out, for instance, that the Buddhist Peace Fellowship, founded in 1978, has done important work on behalf of peace, as have followers of His Holiness the Dalai Lama and the Vietnamese monk Thich Nhat Hanh. But when I ask these friends if their Buddhist sects were founded upon the ideals of peace or social justice as their most basic, fundamental teaching, the answer is invariably no. They may personally endorse those values, and they may belong to a Buddhist group or fellowship that works on behalf of them, but the teachings of their school of Buddhism are not squarely founded upon them. Their Buddhism has not yet been fully reinterpreted for an age of global concerns.

To rouse itself from inertia, it is sometimes necessary for religion to reinvent itself through the work of revolution or reform, and I have no doubt that American Buddhism will do just that, modernizing those teachings that have come to it mostly in premodern form so that they address not just the need for peace of mind or an enhanced immune system but the need for a more equitable distribution of wealth and basic human rights for all. What distinguishes the Soka Gakkai from other

Buddhist traditions in America is that it arrived on U.S. shores in the 1960s with that work largely accomplished. How did the Soka Gakkai accomplish what no other Buddhist school has, either in Japan or anywhere else? How has it managed to "institutionalize" the revolutionary impulse so that, rather than settling back into the predictable mediocrity of a successful religion, it has spread across the globe? What is the driving force that has sustained the Soka Gakkai and preserved its unity as it has traveled to so many other countries and cultures around the world? How has it made the leap from national religious organization to international spiritual movement?

My interest in answering these questions has less to do with the Soka Gakkai itself and more to do with my desire to discover what comes next for religion itself as we transition into a new millennium. For what the Soka Gakkai has discovered isn't just a new form of Buddhism. It's a new way of being religious.

a thing of lasting beauty

No one knows why, but for some reason the founders of religious movements tend to come in threes. Shakyamuni, his disciple Kashyapa, and his cousin Ananda come to mind when we think of ancient Buddhism, while Jesus, Peter, and Paul are representative of Christianity. The three founding presidents of the Soka Gakkai—Tsunesaburo Makiguchi, Josei Toda, and Daisaku Ikeda—follow the same pattern. For there seems to be a natural progression in the creation, development, and stabilization of a new religion, and those three phases each require the talents of individuals with very different temperaments, so that the person who *begins* the movement is very different from the person whose role it is to give it *shape* and *form*, while the person whose work is to *refine* and *extend* its teaching is different still. Probably that is why there are usually three founders. Even at its beginning, religion is a communal effort. We cannot create something of collective value on our own.

The initial founder of a religious movement usually takes great risks. That is the reason why he or she is often persecuted and sometime martyred. Jesus is one example, and if we include philosophical movements as well, Socrates would be another. Tsunesaburo Makiguchi, the first president of the Soka Gakkai, would be yet another. Making a clay pot is a good metaphor to explain how a successful religious movement is created. In the beginning, the process of creation can be quite violent. The clay is usually cut several times—either with a knife or with a wire. Then it must be slapped down hard upon the wheel to give the pot a solid footing. When we think of what this means for the founder of a religious movement, we can see that it takes a special kind of individual to allow himself to be treated that way for the sake of what, in its early stages at least, is mostly just an ideal (the pot is, after all, at this point only a lump of clay). There may be a loose organization in the beginning, a group of committed followers, a meeting schedule, or even a curriculum of sorts; however, once the trouble begins—as it always does—this nearly always falls apart.

On the night that Jesus was taken into custody, his disciples all deserted him. Likewise, when Nichiren incurred the wrath of powerful forces in the military government of his day, only the bravest of his new converts dared stand at his side. How easy it would have been for either man to recant his teachings at this point, letting his disciples off easy and sparing himself injury or even death. For that very reason, there always comes a

moment of truth in the creation of any new religious tradition—a moment when its founder chooses (not for the
sake of what already *is* but for the sake of what *might be*)
to hold firm in the face of persecution, enduring what
he might easily avoid were he merely to shut his mouth.

Tsunesaburo Makiguchi was repeatedly offered his
freedom when he was imprisoned for "thought crimes"
against the Japanese Imperial government during World
War II. Each time he said no. Makiguchi had undergone
a deep religious conversion, an experience the Lotus
Sutra called reaching the "stage of non-regression," the
point in one's spiritual development where it becomes
impossible to turn back and return to the world one
knew before. In Buddhism that old world is sometimes
defined as the world of "upside-down views."

According to the logic of that old, deluded world,
freedom means being at liberty to come and go as we
please. Such a definition of freedom is often very useful to an oppressive regime. That is because freedom, if
so defined, becomes something that can then be taken
away. Tsunesaburo Makiguchi said no when offered his
freedom because the offer itself was deluded. His cap-
tors, who thought *they* were free but in reality were the
"thought prisoners" of an oppressive government and
the victims of a degraded religious culture that had long
since capitulated on the matter of basic human rights,
therefore had nothing to offer him. He was free already.

Like Nichiren before him, his willingness to die for the sake of the Lotus Sutra offered a freedom that could not be taken away by any worldly power or authority. Like Jesus before him (and Nelson Mandela later), Tsunesaburo Makiguchi found in prison something that, given the state of Japanese society during the war, could not be gained outside its walls—true freedom, and with it the power to change the world.

The first founder of any religious movement must find that freedom and that power, and this means that he must be willing to confront the forces of delusion in society—even those forces supported by religious tradition. That means seeing the world right side up and declaring that truth to anyone who will listen. The second founder receives that right-side-up view from his mentor and builds an organization on its principles, declaring and spreading that same freedom and power to a society that, although it may still resist being told the truth, has already begun to accept it on some level. People who are willing to undergo persecution for their beliefs seem more *awake* (and therefore more convincing) than their counterparts in whatever complacent religious culture is then in power. The work of the second founder is still arduous and still not without risk. Likewise, it requires great energy.

Josei Toda's energy in spreading Nichiren Buddhism is almost legendary. When we consider his character—

the fierceness of his resolve to transform postwar Japanese society through faith, plus the creativity and daring he brought to the task of modernizing Buddhism—it is easy to see the hand of a master potter at work. Toda gave the Soka Gakkai the basic shape it has today, a shape that has proven so useful to modern people that it has long since transcended the Japanese culture that gave birth to it and spread to countless other countries across the globe.

We see in the Soka Gakkai, as conceived by Toda, a dynamic and practical philosophy of life that, for the first time in human history, privileges life over religion, rather than religion over life. Toda demanded that the Buddha wake up and be answerable to the lives of ordinary people. He advised his fellow Soka Gakkai members to test the truth of the teachings of Nichiren Buddhism for themselves to see if they actually worked. They did; therefore it spread very quickly and continues to do so nearly sixty years after his death.

But that is not the end of the process, as any potter knows. Even a pot with a very useful shape will not last unless it has been glazed by the potter and then subjected to the prolonged heat of the firing process. Only in this way will the pot become both beautiful and durable enough to survive the constant handling it is likely to encounter in the midst of everyday life.

To the third Soka Gakkai president, Daisaku Ikeda,

fell the task of making the Soka Gakkai a thing of lasting beauty. That phase of creation, like those overseen by his predecessors, was not without its challenges. A man of boundless energy and creativity, Ikeda has accomplished many things over the course of his career, but among those accomplishments, two lie at the heart of his mission.

First of all, Ikeda *internationalized* the teachings of the Soka Gakkai, using them to promote peace, culture, and education in other countries throughout the world. Nichiren Buddhism had always stressed the need to share its teachings widely. In fact, you might say that spreading the teachings of Nichiren Buddhism was the *point* of Nichiren Buddhism. The Lotus Sutra taught that it was by practicing the teachings of that sutra and sharing those teachings with others that one attained the highest wisdom, forging the indestructible happiness of a Buddha for this lifetime and in all lifetimes to come.

From the beginning, Soka Gakkai members were given the same teaching. The surest way to elevate their life condition was to share the movement's message with others, offering them the tools, the teachings, and the supportive spiritual community they needed to take charge of their destinies and improve the overall condition of their lives, their communities, and even society itself. This was what Makiguchi himself taught, and it was the teaching that Toda spread to nearly a million Japa-

nese people in the years immediately following World
War II. But it was still very much focused on Japan and
the struggles of its people. And, after all, it wasn't that
different from what other evangelical religions taught.
Ikeda took Nichiren Buddhism one step further, restat-
ing the Soka Gakkai's mission in terms of human values
that transcended narrow differences of race, religion,
and nationality. By celebrating those values that unite us
all, he empowered the Soka Gakkai with a message that
was, for the first time, truly global. It was Buddhism on a
scale no one had ever seen before. It could go anywhere
and help anyone.

It could also address a whole host of emerging global
issues—problems like climate change, nuclear proliferation, overpopulation, poverty and hunger, and economic expansionism. These were challenges for which the
religious models that had existed up until then did not
adequately prepare us. Only through a process of radical self-empowerment—which Ikeda, expanding upon
a term used by Toda, called Human Revolution—could
human beings address issues that big. They couldn't be
dealt with effectively by any one people, nation, or religion, but only by humanity as a whole. It was Ikeda's
willingness to address such concerns and make them the
main focus of his outreach that transformed the Soka
Gakkai into what may well be the world's first true global
religion.

Ikeda's second undertaking was riskier, as the process of firing always is. For it is always possible that, no matter how functionally perfect the form of a pot is, or how beautifully glazed its surface, it will nevertheless crack during the long process of firing. During that process, the heat must be kept at a constant temperature. Likewise, once that process is over, the cooling must occur naturally. Otherwise, the pot will shatter. During this process it is hidden within the depths of the kiln where the potter cannot see it; he can only proceed with faith that his efforts will be a success. More than anything, he has to *believe* in the whole process. And this is difficult, given the kinds of pressures that the pot is exposed to within the kiln.

Ikeda conducted that "firing" process largely through *dialogue*—with other Soka Gakkai members, with world leaders and scientists, and with an ever-widening circle of artists, writers, and intellectuals from around the world who shared a common concern with peace. Throughout this process, his aim was to refine the teachings of the Soka Gakkai so that it is clear what they stand for and (the importance of this cannot possibly be overstated) what they actually *are*. For the danger of any universal spiritual teaching is that its appeal may be so broad that in the end it cannot hold together and simply falls apart.

In this process, Daisaku Ikeda was aided by the history of the Soka Gakkai itself, which emerged phoenix-like from the ashes of World War II, having endured its dehumanizing deprivations and witnessed its horrors—including the atom bomb. From the beginning, the Soka Gakkai's approach to Buddhism was focused on the fundamental dignity of human life—affirming it, protecting it, and convincing others to do the same. Ikeda's whole philosophy clusters around the word *life*—LIFE with capital letters is how I once heard it described. As a unifying idea at the heart of Ikeda's teachings, it has proved both durable and versatile.

Today, in his eighties, Ikeda continues to extend and develop that idea in dialogue with others, focusing increasingly on the interdependence of life in all of its many aspects, both human and nonhuman species, and the need to protect them all. It's an approach to Buddhism that is almost, but not quite, bigger than Buddhism. You might say that the Soka Gakkai is Buddhism taken as far as Buddhism—or, for that matter, any religion—can go.

the foundation

the creation of the soka gakkai

just one verse of the lotus sutra

I MAGINE A FLAME being passed from candle to candle until fifty candles are lit. It begins with one candle . . . then spreads to fifty. But the flame passed from candle to candle is the same. According to the Lotus Sutra, the spread of Buddhism is accomplished in just this way. It begins when one person hears "just one verse of the Lotus Sutra" and, responding with joy, passes it on to another. From there it is handed along continuously, even to the fiftieth person, without losing any of its force or effect.

In the mid-1990s, while serving as senior editor for *Tricycle: The Buddhist Review,* I proposed a thought experiment to test whether Buddhism could spread around the globe. That test consisted of a single question: Did Buddhism have a teaching that was so universal it could pass quickly from person to person without getting stopped in its tracks, leaping across national, ethnic, economic, and even religious boundaries?

Since then I have had the opportunity to ask probably a hundred different Buddhists, in America and elsewhere, if Buddhism had such a teaching and, if so, what it was.

There was no universal answer. Some held that it was *anatman*, or "not-self," others that is was the doctrine of dependent origination, the basis for the Buddhist belief in karma. Still others claimed that the Buddhist message was impermanence, or interdependence, or consciousness itself. There were those who offered the four noble truths as an answer, and those who recited the name of Amida Buddha, the Buddhist "savior" who welcomed true believers to his heaven-like Pure Land when they died. Devotees of the Dalai Lama told me it was kindness, followers of Thich Nhat Hanh that it could only be "peace with every step." More than one meditator observed that Buddhism was watching the breath, and virtually every Nichiren Buddhist I spoke with told me it was contained in the *daimoku*, or "title," of the Lotus Sutra—Nam-myoho-renge-kyo.

Finally, in 2007 on my second visit to Japan, I found the answer I was looking for. It came from an eighty-seven-year-old war veteran to whom I had not even addressed the question. Instead I'd asked him, "How were you converted?"

In 1953 a family friend had visited Tadashi Murata and told him about a new religious group. "During the war its founders were declared traitors of the nation and sent to prison for opposing the military regime," his friend told him. "That's all I know."

"That's all you know about it?" asked Murata.

"That's all I know," confirmed his friend. "But, good God, man! Isn't that enough? What could be more *certain* than that?"

"And that was when I converted," Murata told me.

I met Murata, along with three women in their eighties, all part of a delegation of Soka Gakkai members who'd been part of the original "Kansai Campaign," a period in the early 1950s when the Soka Gakkai had grown very rapidly, expanding by 11,111 families in the city of Osaka during one month alone. When I asked how they'd joined, I discovered that they'd each been converted by members who had themselves joined the movement only a week or so before.

"But you must have grown up in other religious traditions," I observed. "What made these people approach you like that when they'd only just joined themselves?"

One after another, they explained the "one verse" of the Law that was enough to convert so many people right on the spot, passing from hand to hand like the lit flame of the candle I spoke of earlier. All they'd needed to hear was that the Soka Gakkai put life first. Simple as it was, that was enough to make people want to pass the message along. They'd seen for themselves what happened when religion got the upper hand. Religion served itself. Or it served industry, the military, or the state. In either event, human values—and human *life*—were all but annihilated in the process. The result was a senseless war that had destroyed their own country and much of Asia besides. I observed that this had been the case many times throughout history. The state-sponsored Shintoism that had co-opted virtually every sect of Japanese Buddhism during the war was only one regrettable example. Evangelical Christianity had done the same thing in my country only a few years earlier by supporting the war in Iraq. Religions were always selling out.

That was when I heard Murata's story.

Half a century later, his body still shook with the force of it. "To be called a traitor to the nation during those years, and to hold fast to the truth in spite of everything, what an honor!" he continued, almost shouting now. "There could have been no more honorable title than Enemy of the State!"

I left the interview impressed with what I had heard. Nevertheless, I couldn't help asking myself exactly what truth Murata was referring to. Many people held fast to truth in the face of imprisonment. Persecution was an ordeal and the truth—*some* truth—was essential if one wanted to endure it. But that truth could be anything from Nichiren Buddhism to Aryan Nationalism. Gandhi had held fast to the truth, but then so had the infamous Oklahoma City bomber Timothy McVeigh. There was no guarantee that one's truth would be true for everyone, or that it would even be a truth worth having. In the case of the leaders Murata's friend was referring to, the issue seemed to hinge upon Makiguchi and Toda's refusal to accept a Shinto amulet from the Japanese government, which would have symbolized their patriotism and their willingness to collapse (the government word was "consolidate") their Buddhism under the banner of Japanese militarism. Under the ironically named Peace Preservation Law, prisoners could be detained and interrogated indefinitely for such a refusal.

At one point early on in the transcript of Tsunesaburo Makiguchi's interrogation, he was asked how many amulets to the Sun Goddess Amaterasu and other Shinto deities he had destroyed or caused to be destroyed. Makiguchi's answer was considered so breathtakingly seditious that it bore special mention in the August 1943 edition of *Tokko geppo* (The Special Higher Police Monthly). "We must have burned *at least* five hundred of those things," he'd said. The thought police had little use for him after that, continuing to conduct routine interrogations but without any real conviction that they would change his mind, and Makiguchi died in prison a year later of exhaustion and malnutrition.

Some scholars have insisted that, in refusing to accept

a Shinto amulet, Makiguchi and his disciple Josei Toda were merely adhering to the letter of Nichiren Buddhist orthodoxy, which forbid them from mixing non-Nichiren elements with their religion. According to them, the truth Makiguchi died for was, at best, some version of the right to religious freedom. One Buddhist historian told me it was like the Jehovah's Witnesses refusing to vote or be drawn into politics "because they were citizens of another, higher kingdom." I surprised him by revealing that, in fact, Japanese members of the Jehovah's Witnesses had been imprisoned along with Toda and Makiguchi for their refusal to support the war. There might be something to their higher kingdom after all if it inspired such resistance. Who could say?

But if some scholars questioned the truth of Makiguchi's anti-militarism, his disciples never had. It was a given. Had he been a nationalist, or even religiously indifferent on the matter of the war, he could have secured his release from prison right away. Instead he had died. No. They understood Makiguchi's refusal to accept an amulet in far deeper, far more radical terms.

The truth that had been passed along to Murata from his friend in 1953 was much bigger than the right to religious freedom or some exclusivist approach to Buddhism. It was "certain" in Murata's mind, true, but it wasn't the kind of religious certainty that becomes a weapon in the hands of the ignorant. What was certain for Murata—post-Iwo Jima, post-Nagasaki—was the idea that there had to be a better way for humanity, and that better way could not be delivered by nations, states, or tribes. The truth he spoke of belonged to humanity as a whole, and for that reason it was, indeed, the enemy of the state. It couldn't be used to champion the rights of one group of human beings over another and would even work to subvert such narrow, self-serving impulses. It was truth beyond ethnicity; it was religion reinterpreted for a global age.

understanding our common humanity

FOR MANY YEARS NOW, I have collected amulets such as the ones Makiguchi and his disciples burned, religious trinkets, and talismans from various cultures around the world. These come from every imaginable tradition and are therefore remarkably varied in form. Collectors are drawn to the *particularity* of the things they collect; they think of them as unique or special, and it is that thought that drives the impulse to collect them. For that very reason, however, they tend to overlook the obvious—the ways in which the things they collect are all exactly the same.

Beads, for instance.

Beginning with the rosewood prayer beads I was given the day I became a Zen Buddhist monk, I have collected Catholic rosaries, Orthodox *chotkis*, Buddhist *malas*, and Muslim *tesbih* for half a lifetime now. That is why recently, on meeting a paleoanthropologist who had spent a lot of time excavating in southern France, it occurred to me to ask when beads became prominent in the archaeological record. I was trying to work out a theory about the origins of meditation and prayer.

Beads were among the first human artifacts having a purely decorative function, she explained. "But no, I don't think they originally had anything to do with prayer. They've always existed but became common during the last Ice Age when advancing glaciers pressed early human beings close together in the same habitable region. Beads may have served as a useful visual marker to distinguish one tribe from another. And so you get black bead Homo sapiens and white bead Homo sapiens. Originally, it may simply have been a good way to tell one another apart."

I'd developed a theory that human beings created beads in response to some obscure prehistoric religious impulse (after all, the word *bead* in English originally meant "prayer"). But according to this expert, it was more likely they created them to assert their differences from one another and to evoke the protections and privileges that might come from membership in certain tribes.

Early religions may have had their origins in this same impulse. Prayer and meditation probably came later, as human beings began to confront the simplest truth of all: that tribal affiliation was no protection against the realities of old age, sickness, and death.

That was what the Buddha realized at the beginning

of his spiritual path. According to legend, on the eve of his renunciation, the young prince had four encounters, one at each of the four gates of his palace. At the first gate he encountered an old man, at the second a sick man, and at the third a corpse. Finally, at the fourth gate he encountered a monk, after which he cut his hair, removed his clothes, and left his various amulets and jewels behind, resolving to embrace the life of an ascetic.

The point of the story is not to justify a monastic lifestyle, however, which in itself would have been only another kind of tribe. The monk in the story is Everyman. He is simply an ordinary human being who has grasped the truth about life and suffering and has set his mind on attaining Buddhahood as the only enlightened response. Recently a Facebook friend posted a meme of Dr. Martin Luther King Jr. looking somewhat monkish with his close-cropped hair. Over the photo someone had superimposed a caption: "You don't have to be a Buddhist to be a Buddha."

The Buddha's first realization provided a basis for understanding our common humanity. That is why the community he created abolished the caste system. The Buddha began his teaching by recognizing that the life within each person is fundamentally the same. Today as we enter an age of global concerns, it only makes sense to revisit the foundational simplicity of that first great insight, exchanging our various tribal markers and Buddhist signs of belonging for a flame that can be passed to any other human being on the planet—regardless of ethnicity, race, or religion—in order to bring more light into the world.

I believe this was the kind of Buddhism that Makiguchi was asserting when he refused to "consolidate." That was the religion he died for, and that death, which passed largely unobserved by the world in the darkness of a six-foot square cell, has become a flame that continues to be passed from person to person long after the original candle is gone.

We are now entering a phase of history when we will need all the light we can get, a period when we are once more being "pressed together"—by jet travel, by the Internet, by the global population explosion, the global economy, and eventually (should it have the effect of reducing the habitable land area) by global warming. The old response to that "pressing," in what was probably our species' very first encounter with multiculturalism, was to retreat ever more deeply into the bead-making of tribalism in all its various forms. But that is no longer an option—or not a good option, at any rate.

Barring a global pandemic that reduces the world's population by half, we are not likely to have more space or more natural resources any time soon, as earlier human beings did at the close of the last Ice Age. That being the case, our tribal impulses (along with the competitiveness and lack of cooperation they foster) are sure to pose the gravest danger to humanity. Nuclear proliferation—as grave an issue as that is—is only a symptom of that far deeper problem that human beings must now finally address. That is why, in order to arrive at a suitable message for the coming millennium, Buddhism has reached clear back to its beginnings to reclaim a belief in the fundamental equality and dignity of all life and bring that teaching back to the fore.

As Daisaku Ikeda himself has suggested, a manifesto for the Buddhism of the coming age would therefore be devastatingly simple, for it would consist of only the single word *life,* and all that that it implies: The life and fundamental dignity of each human being and the right to express that life across the entire spectrum of cultural forms. The lives of the many millions of species of plant and animal with which we share this world. Even the life of the earth itself, its mountains and streams, hills and valleys, in all their beauty and diversity.

Like all human beings, Tsunesaburo Makiguchi's experience was rooted in the life and the land of a country he loved, and in the early days at least, in spite of the global scope of his thinking (he was a geographer by training), he felt an affectionate if realistic pride in Japan's national heritage. But then Japan began to fall out of step with human life and human values. Perhaps it was a matter of his waking up one day and realizing that the things he had once believed in were not what they seemed (or never had been), or that they carried far too great a price. That must have been the moment he was asked to accept an amulet. And he couldn't do it.

I find a sad beauty in Makiguchi's words to his interrogators: "We must have burned at least five hundred of those things." They reflect a weariness with amulets and all they signify that has now spread far beyond the confines of Makiguchi's cell. Over and over, humanity destroys them, reasserting the claims of life and the planet, yet somehow they just keep coming back. But, then, there is also reason for hope. Because Makiguchi's words could also be interpreted as a testament of resolve: "I've burned five hundred, and I'd burn five hundred more." That would be the spirit of a new Buddhism. What a great, bright fire so many burning amulets would make.

the power of ideas

I T IS NOT CLEAR whether Tsunesaburo Makiguchi knew that he was laying the foundation for a new paradigm of religious worship when the first volume of his book *The System of Value-Creating Pedagogy* was published on November 18, 1930. He may have ended up as an amulet burner, but he did not begin as one.

On a research trip to Tokyo in 2007, I visited one of the elementary schools, now said to be the finest in Tokyo, where Makiguchi had served as principal. Along the wall of the current principal's office were the portraits and photographs of the school's twenty-five previous heads, from the mid-nineteenth century to the present day, including a now well-known portrait of Tsunesaburo Makiguchi. The photo had only recently been restored to its proper position, I was told. Makiguchi's arrest as an enemy of the state had kept it off the walls for many years. Standing in the principal's office of Shirokane Elementary School, I was struck simultaneously by two contradictory thoughts: That Makiguchi's photo didn't really belong there, and that it did.

Makiguchi alone, among all the principals of Shirokane Elementary, had achieved national fame (and at
one time, infamy) as something other than a school
administrator. Asked if they recognized any of the faces
on that wall as belonging to a person of historical significance, the average Tokyo resident might not pick out
Makiguchi's face every time, but his would doubtless be
recognized far more often than the others.

It wasn't just the fact that Makiguchi had gone on to
found a religious movement. There was another reason
his portrait didn't belong on the principal's wall—the
fact that he had been forcibly transferred, not only
from the Shirokane Elementary School, but from four
other schools as well. Here was a man whose educational
career was devoted to the work of reforming a system
that didn't want reforming—a system which, moreover,
in the decades leading up to World War II, was moving
in the opposite direction.

Tsunesaburo Makiguchi had opposed rote learning,
and although in the beginning he hadn't resisted the
emperor system, accepting it as a distinct and perhaps
even a natural expression of the Japanese character, he
had no interest in an educational system devoted to producing robotic, unthinking servants of the state. Makiguchi had championed the rights of children to learn *as*
children, following the lines of inquiry and curiosity natural to them and learning at their own age-appropriate

pace. And he had placed the *happiness* of children before all else. His entire educational philosophy was based on that fundamental principle, which informed everything he wrote.

That philosophy, which would later merge with the writings of Nichiren Daishonin to form the Soka Gakkai's teachings on Human Revolution, was already well developed before Makiguchi began writing his theories on value-creating education. Standing in the office of the Shirokane Elementary School principal, it occurred to me that Makiguchi's philosophy had been developed in the "human laboratory" of that school and others like it. Call it a growing conviction—that happiness was, or should be, the root concern of human life. That changed everything. But most of all it changed him. The face peering back at me from the wall in the principal's office told the story of a man determined to reform a system and of that system's determination to resist his ideas. His face didn't belong there.

Or perhaps it did, for exactly the same reason. It depended on how you looked at it. His face belonged on the wall precisely because he had resisted a war that had claimed the lives of so many of the young people Makiguchi had taught when he served there. Perhaps Murata was right and it was an honor in those years to be declared an enemy of the state. Society is fickle, and governments often go wrong. And so it sometimes happens that the villains of one generation become the heroes of the next.

The Soka Gakkai marks November 18, 1930, roughly two years after Tsunesaburo Makiguchi's forced retirement from the Tokyo educational system, as the date of its founding. And yet, given that the Soka Gakkai was not formally registered as a religious organization until 1952, this seems a peculiar choice. In a country where the age of a religious sect is typically measured in centuries, the addition of a few years to make it that much older hardly seems worth the effort. Nevertheless, I believe there is a compelling reason to take that earlier date as the real beginning of the Soka Gakkai. The reason is simple: The day Tsunesaburo Makiguchi published *The System of Value-Creating Pedagogy* was the day he first spoke out. That he died in prison for his beliefs exactly fourteen years later on November 18, 1944, makes this all the more poignant.

It is tempting to suggest that the two events might be mystically connected. How else can we explain how the publication of what amounted to little more than a collection of unedited notes on the theory of education set forces in motion that would lead to the death of its author and the creation of a worldwide spiritual revolution?

In a magazine interview I conducted in 2008 with

Daisaku Ikeda, I asked him to comment on the "prophetic" voice in Nichiren Buddhism—its tendency to challenge prevailing authority systems, holding them responsible for discrimination, injustice, or corruption, even when doing so brought along with it certain risks. In response, Ikeda spoke of Nichiren himself:

> Nichiren understood the risks [of challenging the Kamakura-era authorities] and his writings record with great frankness the doubts and questions that assailed him early in his career as he pondered whether or not he should speak out. At one point he confessed to a disciple: "I, Nichiren, am the only person in all Japan who understands this. But if I utter so much as a word concerning it, then parents, brothers, and teachers will surely censure me, and the ruler of the nation will take steps against me. On the other hand, I am fully aware that if I do not speak out I will be lacking in compassion." After a process of intense self-questioning, Nichiren recalled the words of the Lotus Sutra urging that this teaching be spread after the Buddha's passing, and he made a great vow to transform society and enable all people to live in happiness.

In the life of Tsunesaburo Makiguchi we see this same pattern of intensive self-questioning, followed by the firm resolve to speak out. Even so, like Nichiren, the decision was probably a long time in the making.

Makiguchi's theory of value-creating education evolved during his years as an elementary school administrator, the broad outlines of it were there as early as 1903, when he published *A Geography of Human Life*. At that time already, Makiguchi was struggling with what was to become the core problem of the twentieth century—namely, the tension between cultural and global awareness. This conflict is reflected even in the title of the work, which is a kind of paradox in itself.

The title is not a metaphor, as the titles of such books often are today. Nor is it a gimmick. It doesn't indicate that Makiguchi simply intended to discuss human culture in a systematic way, using elements of geography as the organizing principle. *A Geography of Human Life* is a work of geography plain and simple, though one which seeks to situate human life and human culture in relationship to sea, sky, and land. Early on in that work, however, Makiguchi confesses that, although geography itself is quite literally a global discipline, its study must necessarily begin where we are:

> I arrived at a conviction that the natural beginning point for understanding the world we live

in and our relationship to it is that community of persons, land, and culture that gave us birth.

The importance of this passage can scarcely be overemphasized in light of Makiguchi's later theories and the conflicts they inspired, first with educational authorities, and later with the government itself. The first thing to realize is that, as Makiguchi uses it, the idea of "the community of persons, land, and culture which gave us birth" (referred to as "homeland" by other writers of the same era) is so wholesome and so fundamental that it is hard to see how anyone could have felt inspired to challenge it—at least not in 1903. Indeed, *A Geography of Human Life* seems on the whole to have been received with some enthusiasm by the educational community. The idea of homeland was then popular in many countries around the world as a way of recognizing that a single ethnic group had a long history and deep cultural association with a certain geographical area. Even today, the same concept (if not the word) is used to justify the protection of indigenous peoples and their land.

It's worth pointing out, however, that in 1903 there was very little understanding of human origins. It was not widely accepted, as it is today, that human beings had originated in Africa and dispersed only much later to other points around the globe. Therefore, it was still possible for many Japanese people to believe that their emperors had descended from the Sun Goddess Amaterasu, rather than from some common ancestors whose descendents left the African subcontinent approximately seventy thousand years ago—ancestors who have recently been identified by geneticists as the true forebears of all humankind.

At the turn of the twentieth century, there was also nothing approaching a realistic understanding of human destiny or the limits of economic growth. As humanity neared the end of the age of colonial conquest, it experienced a sudden technological explosion—in transportation, in communication, in agriculture, in medicine, in nearly all aspects of life. That explosion literally supersized humanity, extending the influence of those countries who were its masters and expanding the range of human control over the planet and its resources to a level inconceivable to people living only a few decades before.

The availability of cheap effective lighting alone, following Thomas Edison's invention of the incandescent bulb in 1879, greatly extended the range of waking human consciousness, effectively adding more hours onto the day—for work, for entertainment, for study, for discovery, for consumption. Subsequently, one development led to another, and to yet another, fueled by a corporate economy in developed nations, and then later by the arms race, and then the space race, as human ambition literally outgrew the planet. It seemed that there was no limit on what humanity could achieve. But there was a flaw at the heart of that expansive optimism—namely, that humanity cannot exist as a thing apart from nature; it has no destiny but annihilation apart from the land that gave it birth.

I believe that Makiguchi's theory of value has its true origin in the earth, which gives birth to human beings and all other species on the planet, and which works ceaselessly, if naturally, to sustain them and give meaning—and *value*—to their lives. But if this is true, then *homeland* meant something very different to Makiguchi the geographer and the educator from what it has come to mean to us today.

As the twentieth century wore on, the term *homeland* gradually came to be used in fascistic terms. During the lead-up to World War II, the word *Heimatland* was used in propaganda by the Nazi Party, along with its companion term *Vaterland* ("Fatherland"). In fact, the pro-Nazi magazine by the same name, edited by Wilhelm Weiss, was instrumental in that party's rise to power.

Even in America—and in the new millennium no less—the term still expresses a profound ambiguity. Following the events of September 11, 2001, the Bush Administration adopted the name Department of

Homeland Security for its newly founded anti-terrorist agency. But even Republican speechwriter and Reagan biographer Peggy Noonan wasn't comfortable with the term. "The name Homeland Security grates on a lot of people, understandably," she wrote in the *Wall Street Journal* the following June. "*Homeland* isn't really an American word, it's not something we used to say or say now." Noonan warned that the term had "a vaguely Teutonic ring" and suggested that it was likely to get the Republican Party in trouble. She understood that the concept of homeland, with its overtones of isolationism and ethnic solidarity, didn't accord with who Americans thought they were, or who they wanted to be. And, indeed, the election of Barack Hussein Obama, a man of mixed race, mixed religion, and mixed ethnicity, as the forty-fourth president of the United States seemed to suggest something in the nature of a political correction—a nationwide referendum on the whole notion of homeland and what it means to be secure.

In a speech given in March of 2008, Obama delivered what amounted to a short post-tribal declaration:

> I am the son of a black man from Kenya and a white woman from Kansas. I was raised with the help of a white grandfather who survived a Depression to serve in Patton's Army during World War II and a white grandmother who

worked on a bomber assembly line at Fort Leavenworth while he was overseas. I've gone to some of the best schools in America and lived in one of the world's poorest nations. I am married to a black American who carries within her the blood of slaves and slave owners—an inheritance we pass on to our two precious daughters. I have brothers, sisters, nieces, nephews, uncles, and cousins, of every race and every hue, scattered across three continents, and for as long as I live, I will never forget that in no other country on Earth is my story even possible.

Obama's speech on race was played on the Internet millions of times across the globe, making it one of the most watched events in human history and justifying in some measure the claim by one political commentator that its message was intended, not just for Americans, but for people of varied races, histories, and ethnicities across the globe.

But Obama's message could hardly be called American at its core. The America he described in his speech was a kind of nexus point for the post-tribal age—a place where, beginning hundreds of years ago, diverse peoples from across the globe began assembling to forge "a more perfect union." From the beginning that union was fraught with difficulty, and much innocent blood was shed to create and preserve it, but at bottom it was never based on the idea of homeland—the rootedness of one people to one place. Its origin lay in the idea that, having been created equal, people of every race, religion, and national origin could at last come together in one land to find a common home. The "union" it proposed was ultimately a microcosm—a picture in miniature of the globe.

All of this is foreshadowed in *A Geography of Human Life,* and Makiguchi's own life is the story of the gradual but inevitable collision of these two very different ideas of what it means to be at home in the world. These in turn boil down ultimately to the question of what it means to be human, whether that means being a member of a species or only a member of a religion, a nation, or a tribe.

Naturally, some may challenge this view of Makiguchi, and I am the first to admit that my way of reading history relies heavily on the power of ideas—especially progressive ones—to have their way. But I believe that slain civil rights leader Medgar Evers's declaration "you can kill a man, but you can't kill an idea" is more than borne out by history, as the examples of Socrates, Jesus, Gandhi, and Martin Luther King Jr. demonstrate all too well.

opening a way toward the future

WHEN YOU CONSIDER the revolutions of the past, it is easy to see that the one thing they always have in common is violence. Certainly this was true of the American, French, Russian, and Chinese Revolutions. But it is also true when we speak figuratively, as for instance with the Industrial Revolution. Even such a purely historical term calls to mind the massive, sometimes violent upheavals in society necessary to transform an agrarian culture into a manufacturing one. In that process new communities were created, while others were destroyed. Families were separated, sometimes forever, and the land itself was reappropriated for a purpose it had never known before—to be mined, gouged, stripped, and burned. The violent impulse in revolutionary movements is best reflected in the credo of Latin American Marxist revolutionary Che Guevara: "Revolution is not an apple that falls when it is ripe. You have to make it drop."

The term *Human Revolution*, however, points to a very different kind of transformation, precisely because it does not require violence, or condone it. Just the opposite of Guevara's "tree shaking," Human Revolution allows for a process of inner ripening on the part of each individual, and it is this emphasis on individual growth, happiness, and fulfillment—achieved gradually through advances in community, culture, and education—that is at the heart of Makiguchi's theory of value-creating education. Nevertheless, in one respect Guevara's metaphor was apt. Revolution is—or *ought* to be—organic. Because, indeed, its principles are rooted in the land. The question, then as now, is how such a land nurtures human beings, giving rise eventually to the ripe fruit of Human Revolution, rather than inspiring the preemptive tree shaking of war.

The answer goes right to the heart of Tsunesaburo Makiguchi's teachings on value creation, and to the principal method he developed in the 1930s for spreading its message. For it was within the human laboratory of the local discussion group meeting, and the respectful, supportive dialogue it engendered, that Soka Gakkai's new model of religion was ultimately born.

In October 2007 an article appeared in the *Washington Post* reporting the opposition of a neighborhood action group against the construction of an SGI-USA Buddhist culture center on Embassy Row, a prominent area of Washington, D.C. The group's spokesman, John Magnus, claimed that he was not opposed, in principle, to a Buddhist group moving into the neighborhood. After all, the Embassy Row area already hosted the National Cathedral, in addition to a number of other houses of worship. What he disputed was the SGI's claim that its Buddhist culture center was, in fact, a "house of worship." "The [SGI] says that 100 percent of their activities are focused on advancing peace, culture, and education," said Magnus. "Personally, I think that's fabulous. All my neighbors think that's fabulous. It's just not worship."

When I first read this story, I thought it was a simple case of religious discrimination. Had it been a Methodist Church that wanted to build on the same site, the neighbors might still have grumbled about the increased traffic flow, but they would never have dreamed of challenging its status as a bona fide religious organization. Then I remembered an exchange that occurred sometime during the late 1960s between Daisaku Ikeda and a woman whose mother was opposed to her Buddhist practice.

"Do you think your mother would have objected to you joining a religious group other than the Soka Gakkai?" he asked the woman.

"If it had been one of the established Buddhist schools like Pure Land or Zen, I don't think she would mind," was her answer.

"It's not surprising that your mother has some reservations about your practice," admitted Ikeda. "Nichiren

Buddhism is a philosophy on the forefront of the times that is opening the way toward the future."

At bottom, I think this is precisely what Magnus was responding to. A new paradigm always looks unfamiliar. He might have had a harder time mustering opposition to a Zen temple, with its overtly religious architecture and shaven-headed priests, or to a Tibetan Buddhist shrine with monks in maroon robes coming and going through its doors. The SGI has no dress code, no priests or monks, and no identifiable architectural style. It has preserved the substance of the religious life and let the appearance of religion fall away.

What remains when the formality and convention of religious worship have been dispensed with? I believe the answer is really very simple: a concern for basic human values—core *life values* such as peace, happiness, and security; good friends, good food, and good water— that are common to any and all religious traditions of every country around the globe. Perhaps for that reason, to the average person they sometimes don't seem religious anymore. There is nothing about such values that marks them as uniquely Jewish or Christian, Muslim or Buddhist, and nothing that roots them exclusively in the soil of any particular land. They simply reflect what every human being wants and needs. That an ordinary, educated person would think religious worship was something *other* than meeting to share such basic human concerns, to discuss how best to address them in ordinary daily life, and to offer one another encouragement in actually doing so, probably says more about the limits of modern religious education than it does about the Soka Gakkai. There is nothing wrong with the Soka Gakkai's form of worship. The problem lies in the split between religion and life that exists in the minds of most modern educated people.

It was the desire to heal that split which motivated Tsunesaburo Makiguchi to establish the tradition of holding monthly discussion meetings. Once when he was asked whether it might be better to have formal lectures instead of a discussion format, President Makiguchi explained that this would defeat the purpose of meeting to practice Nichiren Buddhism, which empowered individuals to make positive changes in their lives. To accomplish that they had to speak to one another about life's problems through open dialogue, and that would never happen if he just lectured and everybody was sitting there taking notes.

I believe that Makiguchi's response points out a fundamental difference between the old religious paradigm and the new. Really, there is very little difference between a lecture and a sermon. A sermon format, which privileges the authority of the speaker over his or her listeners, is well suited to maintaining conformity in religious settings. (In other words, it is effective in making sure that the religious vision of the lecturer remains the norm.) But it is rarely empowering. By contrast, at a discussion meeting, every voice is heard. Such meetings are egalitarian in spirit, democratic in practice, and decidedly life-affirming in their vision of how Buddhist practice might contribute to the happiness of the individual and, in so doing, provide the foundation for a happy society. "Religion exists to resonate vibrantly within each person," writes Daisaku Ikeda. "Even if one discusses the happiness of all human beings, if it is spoken of apart from the happiness of a single human being, that is mere theory."

There is a deep but simple wisdom in Ikeda's words. Life does not reveal itself in the abstract. Nor is it a collective reality. Life exists in the particular, as it reveals itself in the unique set of circumstances experienced by each individual. Each person exists in a particular place and time, with a wholly unique set of relationships—to family, to society, to the land. Furthermore, the happiness of that individual exists not in the realization of an exalted one-size-fits-all religious or philosophical ideal but rather in the optimization of the life force within them.

As I see it, the primary difference between the SGI and most other contemporary forms of religious worship lies here, in its tradition of openly addressing the challenges to happiness faced by the ordinary individual in the "immediate life context" (or land) they actually inhabit. That difference is so fundamental that I sometimes feel that SGI members don't fully appreciate its implications for the world at large. For what that tradition really offers isn't just a new paradigm of worship for Buddhism but for religion in general. That is because it makes religion answerable to life.

personal transformation through group discussion

A JOURNALIST CONTACTED me a few years ago to ask if I could provide her with a list of individuals who had been inspired by their Buddhist practice to change their lives in some positive way. She wanted to interview "practitioners who were motivated to make a significant change in one specific area of their life as a result of their practice." She gave as possible examples a person who had made a courageous or momentous decision, someone who had triumphed over an addiction, or perhaps one who had moved into social work or some other profession based on the desire to contribute directly to the community they lived in. For the purpose of her article, she defined Buddhist practice as meditation and was therefore primarily interested in talking with practitioners of Zen, Tibetan Buddhism, or *Vipassana* (mindfulness meditation).

I was enthusiastic about the idea of the article, but I warned her that she wasn't likely to get the kinds of responses she was looking for from American meditators.

There was a simple reason for this: their approach to Buddhism was based on age-old models of monastic-style practice that privileged religion over life. Those traditions rarely offered their adherents practical ways of confronting the obstacles and challenges that tended to come up in the course of ordinary life, nor were their communities organized to offer the moral support and inspiration necessary to sustain the kinds of prolonged efforts that are required for real and lasting change at the personal level. The focus of their effort was not on being proactive about life issues and problems but on being religions, albeit in a meditative way. If she asked meditators to provide stories about how they came to this or that spiritual insight, how they passed a certain Zen *koan* or mastered a complex visualization, they were sure to oblige. Ask them how their meditation got them out of a bad job and into a good one, or how it helped them find the right life partner, and they'd probably come up blank.

In fact, that had been the case. She confessed that, so far, she had received not one story of the kind she'd been looking for. Although they might have lowered their blood pressure or their stress level, or enhanced their immune system or their powers of concentration, the meditators she interviewed could draw no direct line of influence between their practice and overcoming the challenges and obstacles to growth that people ordinarily struggled with in life. There was little sense that devoting themselves wholeheartedly to their Buddhist practice had led directly to any *specific* positive outcome in their lives. That was why she had contacted me for advice.

In the end, I told her she was right to challenge American Buddhists to show actual proof of the benefits of meditation practice. While she was waiting for them to do that, however, there was no reason she shouldn't visit an SGI discussion meeting in her neighborhood. There she would discover that chanting practice, coupled with monthly study and discussion meetings, provided inspiration and support for just the kinds of positive life changes she was talking about. "Go to virtually any discussion meeting in the Boston area," I told her, "and you'll hear at least one or two inspiring stories of personal transformation."

A week later, she wrote to me again. On the advice of the SGI-USA representative I'd put her in touch with, she'd contacted a woman, a well-known musician, who had a deeply inspiring story to tell. It turned out that she'd interviewed the same woman once before, though for an entirely different article, and had liked her immediately. She was surprised to find that she was also a longtime SGI member. That, it turned out, was the back story to her successful musical career. I wasn't surprised by this at all. Based on years of watching the Soka Gakkai in action and listening to its members tell their stories, that's what happened when you held Buddhism accountable for changing your life. Although, by modern standards, it seems an extremely simple and obvious notion that religion should serve life, it is nevertheless an utterly revolutionary idea. The monthly discussion meeting is "where the rubber meets the road," Buddhism is put to the test, and the truth of its teachings are manifested by members through personal stories of overcoming obstacles to happiness. Sharing such experiences builds faith, faith builds lives, and collectively those lives can change society. As Daisaku Ikeda has written, "A great human revolution in just a single individual will help achieve a change in the destiny of a nation and further, will enable a change in the destiny of all humankind."

It is often said that the Soka Gakkai's teachings on Human Revolution begin with its second president, Josei Toda, and it is true that Toda gave those teachings their definitive form, but in Tsunesaburo Makiguchi's life, and in his development of a post-tribal model for religious transformation through group discussion, we can see those teachings already dynamically at work in the world.

the development

the discovery of modern buddhism

religion serving life, not life religion

"**M**AKIGUCHI IS DEAD." These were the words, spoken by a prison official on January 8, 1945, with which Josei Toda learned of the death of Tsunesaburo Makiguchi two months earlier. Until that moment, the future second president of the Soka Gakkai hadn't realized that his mentor had died.

According to Toda, when he heard those words, he "just stood there stunned, unable even to weep. . . . I had never experienced such grief as I felt at that moment. Then and there, I resolved: I will show the world. . . . I will achieve something great to repay him."

Moved as he was, however, Toda would never have made good on his vow if not for two other events that had occurred in his life the year before.

The first, in early March 1944, was his sudden discovery in prison that "the Buddha was life itself," the experience of enlightenment that later formed the basis for his radically modern reinterpretation of the Lotus Sutra.

If a truth is profound and deeply felt, it can be stated

very simply. And if it can be stated simply, it is useful. This fact has been understood by reformers throughout the ages—from Shakyamuni Buddha to Jesus of Nazareth to Martin Luther King Jr. Using this criteria, it is hard to imagine a simpler, more profound, or more useful truth than the one arrived at in March 1944 by Toda as he struggled with a passage from the Immeasurable Meanings portion of the threefold Lotus Sutra.

According to the Immeasurable Meanings Sutra, the body of the Buddha was

> neither existing nor not existing,
> neither caused nor conditioned, neither self nor
> other,
> neither square nor round, neither short nor long,
> neither appearing nor disappearing, neither
> born nor extinguished . . .

The passage went on to include eight more lines, offering a total of thirty-four negations in all. The Buddha's body was neither this nor that, the sutra explained. But it didn't say what it *was*.

As many times as Toda had read this passage, he still could not understand it. And yet the Immeasurable Meanings Sutra served as a kind of "introduction" to the Lotus Sutra. If Toda wanted to understand the Lotus Sutra, as he had vowed to do, it only stood to reason that he had to understand this part first. But no matter how he struggled, the body of the Buddha would not reveal itself to his mind.

In truth, he was stuck. There seemed to be no way forward unless he could understand this one fundamental point. "In a sense, he burned the bridges behind him in the battle to understand the Lotus Sutra," said Daisaku Ikeda of the first great spiritual struggle of Toda's life. In other words, like his mentor before him, Toda had reached the point of non-regression, the point of resolve beyond which it was no longer possible to turn back.

Where Buddhism is concerned, it is probably fortunate that Josei Toda was incarcerated by the Japanese government during World War II. Had he been allowed his freedom, there is no guarantee that he would have studied the sutra so fiercely. Even had he felt inspired to do so, with access to the countless commentaries and scholarly resources on the Lotus Sutra that would have been available to him as a free man, it is unlikely he would have felt so driven to forge his own understanding of what he read.

When I visited the original site of Josei Toda's tutorial school in Shinagawa Ward, Tokyo, which is said to be the birthplace of the Soka Gakkai, I asked the curator there about Toda's activities before the war. I was told that he handled the money end of President Makiguchi's various projects, contributing his writing and editorial skills to the fledgling Soka Kyoiku Gakkai (Value-Creating Education Society). When I asked how involved Toda had been in the more spiritually oriented discussions and meetings, however, my guide humorously recalled a scene from the film *The Human Revolution* in which Toda, who was mostly concerned with the business side of things, is shown drinking sake out on the porch during Makiguchi's discussion meetings.

This portrait of Toda before World War II agrees completely with my estimation of him as a man—practical, with a no-nonsense approach to life and commerce and little interest in spiritual matters that could not be proven to have a direct impact on life. Such people often feel like outsiders in religious circles. But the persecutions of the Soka Gakkai during World War II changed Toda permanently, driving him deep within himself.

Still, there must have been something of the porchsitting, sake-drinking Toda even in prison, because he tried several times to send his copy of the Lotus Sutra home to his family. But each time, mysteriously, without any explanation, it was returned to his cell. It was as if the Lotus Sutra belonged there. As if it were waiting for him to finally open it and see what he could discover there. Finally, Toda understood that it was his destiny to study it—even though, being of such a practical mindset, at first he could not see how it was relevant to his condition. And so, beginning on January 1, 1944, in the first of countless determinations that Toda would make as part of his commitment to the process of Human Revolution, he resolutely plunged ahead.

It was sometime in March of that same year, after having read the complete sutra through three times, that Toda began to ask himself what constituted the body of the Buddha. He reasoned that it was neither the physical body of Shakyamuni nor merely an abstract idea with no substance. In the first case, such a body—the product of countless lifetimes of ascetic practice—was unattainable by the average human being. In the second, it was mere idealism, a religious fantasy with no practical value for ordinary life.

According to *The Human Revolution*, Daisaku Ikeda's novelistic history of the Soka Gakkai, finally one day as Toda was chanting Nam-myoho-renge-kyo in his cell, he entered a state of deep meditation, "recalling each of the thirty-four negations one after the other—trying to imagine what it might be that could absolutely exist despite so many negational words." Eventually, he lost track of how long he had been chanting and finally even forgot where he was. It was then that a single word flashed suddenly through his mind: Life. There was nothing mystical or mysterious about it at all, he finally realized. The Buddha was life itself.

What did the identity of the Buddha as life itself mean for Toda, and for modern people in general?

In a word, it meant "freedom." It meant that the
authoritarian interpretations of Buddhist texts that for
hundreds of years had ruled people's understanding of
their religion could at last be shaken off. Because if the
primary reference point for understanding Buddhism
lay in the life force of each individual rather than in the
opinions of learned priests and monks, that meant that
Buddhism was truly accountable to the individual. Prior
to Toda there always existed a gap between the concerns
of Buddhism and those of daily life. One might have
recourse to a wise priest or teacher who demonstrated
that the two could sometimes be brought into harmony,
but for the most part religion was a kind of "professional
sport." Only if you separated yourself from ordinary day-
to-day struggles of working and raising a family—by living in a monastery or a temple, for instance—could you
hope to make the lofty spiritual ideals of Buddhism a
reality in your life. Buddhism was for the priest or monk.
Ordinary people simply got by as best they could.

Josei Toda's great insight was to put life first, not religion, in effect inverting the traditional hierarchical structure of Buddhism, which placed spiritual authority in
the hands of a religious or intellectual elite. That is why
it was inevitable from the beginning—and even necessary—that the Soka Gakkai would eventually experience
a break with its priestly parent organization, Nichiren
Shoshu. To put life first, as Josei Toda did, meant that

each member of the future Soka Gakkai would be connected directly to the Buddha without the mediation of any "professional" religious class committed to its own prosperity and security rather than to the happiness of those it served.

It was this realization that must have lead to the second spiritual breakthrough of Toda's prison years, which occurred a few months later—coincidentally, on almost the exact same day as Makiguchi's death, although Toda did not realize this at the time. That breakthrough took the form of a mystical vision in which Toda found himself among the "Bodhisattvas of the Earth" from the Lotus Sutra and realized that he must be one of them.

In Buddhism, a bodhisattva is a being who resolves to be reborn perpetually in order to save all sentient beings from suffering—as opposed to committing him or herself to the goal of nirvana, a "blown-out" state in which all desires are extinguished and life itself is transcended, which was the aim of early Buddhism. Since Buddhism taught that sentient beings were numberless, that basically meant that the bodhisattva, who committed to a life of eternal service, cultivating vast reserves of energy, wisdom, and compassion, was on a quest as big as the universe itself.

The Lotus Sutra is filled with all kinds of Buddhist followers who have assembled to hear its teachings—including bodhisattvas, who appear in the assembly alongside the Buddha's ordinary monks and nuns. But until halfway through the sutra none of them have ever seen or even heard of the Bodhisattvas of the Earth. The Buddha announces that he has entrusted the task of preaching the Lotus Sutra in an age to come to these very beings, and at that moment the world shakes and cracks open and millions of these Earth Bodhisattvas appear. The Buddha's other followers are astounded. How could Shakyamuni have converted so many millions of bodhisattvas in the brief span of his life?

That question foreshadows the revelation, made in the next chapter of the Lotus Sutra, that the Buddha doesn't enter extinction as people once believed, attaining nirvana and thereafter effectively disappearing from the world. Like the life force that Toda understood earlier while meditating in his cell, the Buddha is eternally present, manifesting as the limitless energy and creativity of the universe itself.

To find himself in the company of the Bodhisattvas of the Earth, transported directly into the mythic world of the Lotus Sutra, seems an uncharacteristic vision for a hard-nosed, practical-minded man like Toda who had had little interest in such mystical affairs. But in retrospect, the vision fit the man. Toda understood that the Bodhisattvas of the Earth in whose company he found himself were none other than ordinary people living and struggling in the world. *These* were the people the teachings of the Lotus Sutra were designed for. Unlike other Buddhist teachings, which emphasized a monastic-style practice that could be mastered by few, the Lotus Sutra taught that ordinary individuals could attain Buddhahood in this life. . . . Because Buddhahood *was* this life.

Josei Toda emerged from his vision convinced that the Bodhisattvas of the Earth spoken of in the Lotus Sutra were none other than members of the Soka Gakkai. Later, the Nichiren Shoshu priesthood that originally sponsored the movement would marvel at how fast the Soka Gakkai grew, winning more new converts in a few decades than the priesthood had in centuries. But Toda understood it perfectly well. Had not Shakyamuni explained to his ordained disciples in the Lotus Sutra that it was these ordinary Earth Bodhisattvas—laypeople to a one—who were entrusted with the sacred duty of spreading Buddhism around the world?

There is something deeply poignant, and at the same time strangely appropriate, about the fact that Toda's vision and Makiguchi's death took place within a day of one another in November 1944. The two experiences are polar opposites. Toda's vision of the Bodhisattvas of the Earth was a transcendently joyful and life-affirming occasion, whereas the death of his mentor plunged him headlong into the deepest grief he had ever known. And yet, I believe those events mark the precise moment when the two great teachings of the Soka Gakkai first came together in a single person and the resolve to build the movement into what it is today was born.

Without Toda's revelation that the Buddha is life itself, and his vision of the Bodhisattvas of the Earth that completed it, Makiguchi's death would almost certainly have crushed his hope for the future. Likewise, without the death of his mentor, those revelations (extraordinary as they were) might have lacked the urgency that drove Toda to spread the Soka Gakkai's teachings throughout Japan.

Daisaku Ikeda explains it in terms of an event from the Lotus Sutra called the "Ceremony in the Air," during which the Buddha and his entire assembly of followers ascends into the heavens above the mountaintop where he has been delivering the sutra, transcending the world of ordinary concerns and—for the moment, at least—attaining a panoramic view of the cosmos.

> From real life to the Ceremony in the Air and then back to real life—this continuous back-and-forth process is the path of human revolution, the path of transforming our state of life. . . . We can change nothing unless our feet are firmly planted on the ground.

The discovery of Makiguchi's death marks the first pairing of religious idealism with firm, practical resolve that distinguished Toda's career as a religious leader and that has virtually defined the Soka Gakkai movement ever since.

glimmers of a global movement

THE MEANING of certain events in collective human history is clear from the moment they happen. A ship is sunk, and a war begins. After years of careful planning, a human being sets foot on the moon. The significance of personal events, however, usually emerges only with the benefit of hindsight. This is especially true when we speak of the hardships or tragedies. By their very nature, such events interrupt the course of individual lives, forcing us to reevaluate ourselves—our goals, our values, even our sense of who we are.

On August 23, 1950, having already failed in business the previous year when his publishing company was forced to close, Josei Toda suspended operations of the credit association of which he'd become director the year before. In the shadow of a government investigation, and with legal action against him seemingly inevitable, Toda voluntarily stepped down from his position as general director of the Soka Gakkai, a post he had held for more than twenty years. His motive was to prevent negative associations with the still-fragile postwar organization. Added to Toda's disappointment over his failed business ventures and the constant harassment of creditors was the knowledge that a number of Soka Gakkai members had invested heavily in the association and some suffered financial hardship because of its failure. Some even left the movement as a result.

Toda remained generally optimistic in his attitude toward business matters (the economic climate in postwar Tokyo was, after all, extremely volatile and fraught with risk). But he became deeply reflective about his relationship to the teachings of Nichiren Buddhism, unwilling (or perhaps unable) to go forward in his spiritual life until he had asked himself the most penetrating questions. Naturally, the most urgent of these questions concerned the role of business in his spiritual life.

From the earliest days of the Soka Gakkai, Toda had assumed responsibility for the financial viability of the organization, often funding its operations and outreach programs out of his own pocket. "Therefore, when he dedicated himself to the reconstruction of the organization after the war," writes Ikeda, "he first gave consideration to the establishment of its economic foundation rather than its organizational development." This strategy made sense while Makiguchi was alive; Toda's writing and publishing efforts allowing the older man to concentrate on pursuing his educational reforms. But now he began to wonder if, all along, this strategy hadn't been a way of avoiding responsibility for the *spiritual* leadership of the organization.

If it is true that new religious movements typically follow three stages in their years of formative growth—foundation, development, and completion—and that in each stage of growth a leader emerges whose temperament and abilities match the demands of the movement at that particular stage, then it is clear that Josei Toda was continuing to build a foundation for the Soka Gakkai, when it was actually the development and rapid expansion of the organization that was being called for.

Josei Toda showed a dynamic entrepreneurial spirit as a businessman and, given the right economic climate, had the skills to succeed as a businessman. Nevertheless, it is difficult to imagine anyone remarking years after Toda's death that he had been unusually gifted in that field, that there had been no other businessman of his caliber during the years of economic reconstruction. And yet, today even those who are critical of Josei Toda and the Soka Gakkai are forced to concede that, when we consider those religious leaders who rose to prominence immediately following World War II, Toda has no equal. He was the most innovative, most dynamic, most successful religious leader of his day.

The second period in the formation of the Soka Gakkai—the period of development—rightly begins when Toda resolved to succeed Makiguchi, becoming the organization's second president. According to Toda, that resolve occurred when he realized that other new religious groups had experienced dramatic growth during the mid-twentieth century, while the Soka Gakkai had not. Toda blamed himself for this and made a public vow to spread the teachings of Nichiren Buddhism to 750,000 families before he died. His fulfillment of that vow had much to do with the core idea behind the Soka Gakkai—that of religion serving life. It was a message with tremendous urgency in postwar Japan, as people sought the vitality and the sense of hope necessary to rebuild their lives and their nation. Toda's decision to make the spread of that "viral message" the principal activity of the movement allowed the Soka Gakkai to spread by the force of its own intrinsic appeal.

All that remained was for Toda to set that message in motion. When he announced his determination to increase the movement's ranks to 750,000 families during his lifetime in his inaugural address of May 3, 1951, most people felt it was an impossible goal to fulfill. The Soka Gakkai membership at that time stood at just a little more than three thousand individuals. The fact that Toda was able to convince the membership even to embrace such a goal is a testament to his powers of persuasion. But there is more at work here than the charisma of a single individual. What Toda seems to have felt within himself—and was therefore able to communicate to others—was the sense that the Soka Gakkai had been entrusted with a special mission to spread the teachings of Nichiren to a struggling nation. At the back of his mind, however, he must have felt glimmers of the global movement that ultimately developed from that national mission. This is made clear by his desire, shortly before his death on April 2, 1958, to spread the teachings of Nichiren Buddhism to the rest of the world. However, nowhere is this broader concern with humanity as a whole more clear than in his declaration of September 8, 1957, proposing the worldwide ban of nuclear weapons.

a global spiritual shift

IN 1946, the year following the world's first use of nuclear weapons, Albert Einstein declared, "The unleashed power of the atom has changed everything save our modes of thinking." Sadly, nearly seventy years later, this is still the case. The discovery of nuclear energy represented a radical shift in the paradigm that until then had governed scientific theory and practice, but there was no corresponding shift at a social or spiritual level to prepare humanity for the awesome responsibility that came with unprecedented destructive power. A widening chasm opened before us that, then as now, seems almost impossible to bridge.

Fortunately, what seems impossible at the level of society (namely, a global spiritual shift to keep pace with the rapid scientific one) is nevertheless possible at the level of the individual, and so there is reason for hope. As Daisaku Ikeda has written: "A great human revolution in just a single individual will help achieve a change in the destiny of a nation and further, will enable a change in the destiny of all humankind."

In retrospect, I believe this "human revolution in just a single individual" is precisely what we see happening on September 8, 1957, when Josei Toda gave his famous declaration calling for the abolition of nuclear weapons.

Brief as it is, the text of that declaration sounds as shocking today as it did when it was delivered more than half a century ago. A shift in paradigm is always shocking. At first we can't be certain we have heard it correctly. Because it transcends old ways of thinking, it is difficult to assimilate. In the beginning, we lack the spiritual and intellectual resources for taking it in. Indeed, we may feel tempted to reject a new paradigm at first because it doesn't fit our way of thinking.

On that day, before a stadium of fifty thousand youth members of the Soka Gakkai, Toda stated what he hoped his listeners would regard as his "foremost instruction for the future." Given that he was then already ill—indeed, he would die seven months later—his words must have carried the added power of a last will and testament. In the famous photograph taken of him on that occasion, sporting a giant chrysanthemum on his lapel, it is clear that his physical vitality is on the wane. But he was making a transmission of the teaching he had devoted his life to, and he did so in the strongest and most uncompromising of words:

> Although a movement calling for a ban on the
> testing of nuclear weapons has arisen around

the world, it is my wish to go further, to attack the problem at its root. I want to expose and rip out the claws that lie hidden in the very depths of such weapons. I wish to declare that anyone who ventures to use nuclear weapons, irrespective of their nationality or whether their country is victorious or defeated, should be sentenced to death without exception.

Even his successor and closest disciple, Daisaku Ikeda, had to struggle to grasp the meaning of Toda's words, and so it goes without saying that they were not immediately understandable to everyone assembled for his address. For one thing, Buddhism does not support the idea of a death penalty. For another, Toda himself had often spoken out against it, claiming the idea of capital punishment was "absolutely futile."

Toda's declaration was one of those occasions when a spiritual leader seeks to shock us out of our ordinary way of thinking. In Toda's case, what he wanted to communicate was an entirely new way of living in human society, one that would prove necessary if we were to survive in a global age.

That new way of living was based on an awareness of the fundamental dignity of human life. But to attain that awareness, one first had to identify oneself as fundamentally *human* rather than being merely a member of a nation, a religion, or a tribe.

At the beginning of his life mission, when Josei Toda stated his value-creating philosophy with the simple words "the Buddha is life itself," he did not mean that the Buddha's life was the life of a person living in Japan. Though in the beginning his mission was directed toward the impoverished and downtrodden people of postwar Japan, it was never restricted to purely nationalistic concerns. It was simply the right place to start—with his own devastated country and his own suffering people. But from the beginning, his religious vision broke the tribal mode. Even in his later struggles with various adversaries—with the Nichiren Shoshu hierarchy and with the Japanese government—he was aware that the true nature of his struggle was with "the claws of evil" hidden in the depths of the human heart itself. This was his only adversary in life, and in truth the only real adversary of humanity itself. When he called for the death penalty for anyone who ventured to use weapons of mass destruction, he was calling for all of humanity to unite in resisting the only force that could possibly destroy them—the roots of the three poisons: greed, anger, and ignorance.

These were the hidden claws in the depths of the human heart that needed to be eradicated. They needed to be ripped out. They actually needed to be sentenced to death. Buddhism has sometimes been criticized for its arms-length approach to the problem of evil. In fact, religious scholars sometimes question whether Buddhism, which shows such sober, analytical detachment on the issue, has any doctrine of evil at all. But Toda's Buddhism had no such problem. He wasn't afraid to identify evil or to grapple with it. In his cell in Toyotama Prison, he had grasped the fundamental life force of the universe, an energy that existed equally in the life of every individual and therefore affirmed the dignity and value of all. To champion that dignity in the world—not just as a religious theory but *actively*—meant being willing to engage with its opposite. That opposite was the bomb. For what is a nuclear warhead—even when it is stockpiled—if not the ultimate symbol of a heartless and indifferent attitude toward life? Could you be enlightened without being awake to the presence of such an "enemy"? Could you be a Buddha and sleep soundly while thousands of warheads were poised and waiting, pointed at human beings all across the globe?

In making his declaration calling for the abolition of nuclear weapons, Toda called for all humanity to unite, crossing traditional boundaries of tribe and country, victor and vanquished, in opposing a force that was truly the enemy of all. It was the first time in human history that the shape and contour of that enemy had become fully apparent. Until then, human beings had always been content to war among themselves, satisfied with the traditional notion of "enemy as other." Now, for the first time, they faced an enemy with the power to destroy them all.

At first it must have seemed to Toda's listeners that he was talking about the scientists who had developed such weapons, or politicians who had authorized their use, or perhaps the soldiers who had deployed them. But they quickly realized that the real enemy, whom Toda referred to as "a devil incarnate, a fiend, a monster," was much vaster and more powerful than that. Storm the palace or the presidium and you might find its minions, but the demon itself could be found only by searching out the deepest recesses of the human psyche. This enemy was far more dangerous than any single nation, territory, or tribe. That was because it had the power to destroy *all* nations, *all* territories, and *all* tribes—and given the freedom to exercise its influence over humanity, it was almost certain to do exactly that.

In retrospect, the new paradigm bequeathed by Josei Toda to his successor, Daisaku Ikeda, and to the rest of the Soka Gakkai youth was more than an antidote to the single problem of nuclear proliferation. In truth, Toda was offering the solution to all other manner of global problems—from terrorism to economic expansionism to global climate change. For none of these problems can even be addressed unless men and women across the globe become empowered as individuals through a process like Human Revolution. Only a paradigm that expands their vision beyond the traditional boundaries separating human beings and defining their interests apart from one another can possibly address problems that exist on a truly global scale.

The advent of nuclear weapons brought with it the necessity for a new way of thinking. For the first time in history, human beings became capable of destroying all human life. Likewise today, the problem of global climate change cannot be solved by nationalities or special interest groups acting alone. Global problems require global solutions, even though they must be implemented locally. And global solutions require a global consciousness—and the willingness of all humanity to work together as one. But as with all radical shifts in consciousness, it has to begin somewhere. In Buddhism, I believe we can trace that beginning to September 8, 1957.

passing the flame of reform

TODA'S HEALTH deteriorated rapidly in the months following his anti-nuclear declaration until his death in a Tokyo hospital on April 2, 1958. But his diminished vitality seemed to sharpen his resolve. In his final decisions as leader of the Soka Gakkai we can find a much more discerning sense of mission, as though certain problems had become perfectly clear to him only with his passing of the torch.

The first was his decision to remove those Soka Gakkai leaders who routinely used the organization for their own monetary benefit. In the early days, some leaders took advantage of their influence among a rapidly growing membership to peddle insurance policies and other goods and services. The sheer size of the Soka Gakkai, Toda observed, virtually ensured that it would attract a certain number of parasites who, if left unchecked, would devour the organization from within. The second was to eliminate the system of allowing "courtesy positions" to certain individuals, rather than awarding such leadership roles based on effort and ability. These recommendations were instantly followed, resulting in the dismissal of forty-six leaders on March 28, less than a week before Toda's death.

These were reasonable recommendations that came as a relief to most of the members. But their real significance lies in the fact that both were safeguards against stagnation. Having passed the flame of the Soka Gakkai's teachings on to its younger members, Toda was concerned about any problems within the organization that might lead to it going out. For there are only two ways a candle flame can be extinguished. The first is when a wind or some other force acts upon it. Toda had taken precautions against this already by building a very strong "housing" for his flame in the structure of the Soka Gakkai itself. The second was more dangerous, however, and far more insidious. That is because it simply involved letting the candle continue to burn. For even if no other force acted against it, eventually the wax would be exhausted, and the candle would go out. The only protection against this second danger was continuous outreach—spreading the teaching to others, "even to the fiftieth person," to see how far it would go. The flame must be continuously passed along.

It was this last problem that Toda wrestled with and sought to address by ensuring that the Soka Gakkai leadership would remain actively involved in spreading the teachings of Nichiren Buddhism instead of degenerating into a commercial or authoritarian structure—a destiny that is almost inevitable in religious organizations of a certain size, unless measures are taken to prevent it. Sharing the practice with others was already integral to Nichiren Buddhism; thus Toda felt doubly justified in making it the principal aim of the Soka Gakkai going forward. But it served a practical purpose as well. Toda's genius lay in the bringing together of just these two considerations—the spiritual and the practical—and joining them as one. His spiritual journey may have had its beginning in the "Ceremony in the Air" of the Lotus Sutra, but over the course of that journey, true to the spirit of a Bodhisattva of the Earth, his feet never left the ground.

It was this practical spirituality that Toda passed along to Daisaku Ikeda, the young man he met in August 1947, who became his closest disciple and confidant for the remainder of his life. According to Ikeda, Toda spoke to him a number of times during his final days about the need to spread Nichiren Buddhism beyond the shores of Japan. Then, sometime in late March 1958, just a week or so before he died, Toda woke from a dream in which he had arrived in Mexico to find many people waiting for him. "I want to go," he said enthusiastically but then quickly recovered his wits, reminding Ikeda, and perhaps himself as well, that the younger man would have to complete that mission. A while later, having given the matter more thought, he said to Ikeda: "The world is your challenge; it is your true stage. It is a vast world. There are many peoples, many races. Some nations are democratic and some socialist. And religious beliefs differ from country to country as well. Some do not permit religious propagation. We'll have to start thinking about how to disseminate the Mystic Law in such places. After all, realizing peace and happiness for humanity is the fundamental aim of Buddhism." Toda left in Ikeda's hands a national organization on the verge of going global—an organization which, moreover, would *have* to spread globally in order to remain healthy and fulfill its greater mission. But there remained one urgent matter to attend to before Toda could die in peace.

That the Soka Gakkai's teachings were too big for any one country to contain—including Japan—was clear to Toda by the end of this life. Human Revolution was a model of spiritual practice that could—and *should*— spread around the world to whoever could benefit from it. But there remained one barrier to spreading those teachings outside of Japan. That was the Nichiren Shoshu priesthood which, until that time, had served as the Soka Gakkai's "anchor" to traditional Buddhism in Japan.

In the beginning that anchor was necessary. It provided continuity with the past through ritual and through its focus on the teachings of Nichiren. Its temples also served as meeting places for larger Soka Gakkai gatherings. And, then, both Makiguchi and Toda had become converts to Nichiren Shoshu Buddhism at the beginning of their respective paths. Each reinterpreted the Lotus Sutra-based teachings of Nichiren Buddhism in ways that the priesthood would never have dreamed of, especially to the degree they used those teachings to empower lay people to think and act for themselves. Nevertheless, there was a real connection—at least in the beginning. But there was no way that connection could last.

The truth is, *no* traditional religious organization could have maintained its connection to the Soka Gakkai as it grew and spread. The Soka Gakkai's teachings on individual self-empowerment, coupled with a model of practice centered on discussion meetings, would have broken free of virtually *any* school of Buddhism. Had Zen or Pure Land Buddhism resisted the forces of wartime fascism and evolved a paradigm like the Soka Gakkai's, the result would have been exactly the same. Implicit to the Soka Gakkai's ongoing critique of the Nichiren Shoshu sect is an idea that Nichiren Shoshu and the Soka Gakkai could have remained one had the priesthood behaved in a more virtuous manner—had it been less grasping, less obsessed with exerting priestly control over the activities of the lay organization. The problem with this view is its failure to recognize that the Soka Gakkai, in following the first stirrings of an inclusive, humanitarian-based global ethic, had broadened the idea of religious virtue to such a degree that the priesthood could no longer understand it. Virtue was no longer a matter of properly tending to rituals and rules of a priestly religion. In fact, it involved forgoing a lot of outworn rules and ritual in order to spread the teaching more widely than ever before. There was no way that a small priestly sect was going to give up control over an increasingly prosperous and influential lay group without a fight, nor could it exert much influence over a group thousands of times its size, especially one that grew as fast as the Soka Gakkai. They'd never have been able to keep up. Nichiren Shoshu finally solved the problem in 1991 with a preemptive strike, excommunicating the Soka Gakkai's entire membership, an act that a religion professor friend of mine once compared to the flea divorcing the dog.

Jesus of Nazareth, who once initiated a new religious paradigm of his own, described the inevitable war between the new and the old in this way:

> And no one pours new wine into old wineskins. If he does, the wine will burst the skins, and both the wine and the wineskins will be ruined. No, he pours new wine into new wineskins. (Mark 2:22)

All of which suggests that there are deeper and far more powerful spiritual and historical forces at work in the separation of the Soka Gakkai from Nichiren Shoshu. After all, it was only when the Soka Gakkai slipped the cultural moorings of traditional Nichiren Buddhism that it was able to travel to 192 other countries around the globe.

It's all there, in Josei Toda's words to the young Ikeda, "The world is your challenge." He might have added that that world, and the Soka Gakkai's proper relationship to it, was a profound and puzzling enigma Ikeda would have to solve.

the completion

the spread of religious humanism

waking the buddha

O N AUGUST 14, 1947, ten years to the day before I
was born in a small town called Mexico, Missouri,
Daisaku Ikeda met Josei Toda for the first time. When I
first discovered the date of that meeting, and then learned
of Toda's dying wish to travel to Mexico, I reflected on
the humorous coincidence. The tiny town of my birth
was, of course, not the Mexico of Toda's dream, and
the image of those 1950s Missouri "Mexicans" waiting in
rapt anticipation for the arrival of Nichiren Buddhism
was unlikely to say the least. Nevertheless, I couldn't
help wondering if, as the result of Daisaku Ikeda's tire-
less efforts to internationalize the movement, sixty years
later the Soka Gakkai International hadn't spread even
there. How far could it go?

Out of curiosity I called a friend at the SGI-USA head-
quarters in Santa Monica, California, to ask if, in fact, the
Soka Gakkai had ever penetrated that deep into small-
town Christian America. A few hours later, I heard from
a local chapter leader in Columbia, Missouri, who told
me that an SGI-USA member had been born in Mexico,

Missouri, and moved back there for some years to be with his elderly mother, only to be joined later by Brazilian members who had emigrated to the United States. And so the answer was yes. Nam-myoho-renge-kyo had been chanted twice daily in Mexico, Missouri, and the teachings had almost certainly been shared with others in its homes and workplaces. Having observed the SGI and its members for some years already, none of this surprised me very much. Once you start lighting one candle with another, there is no limit to how far the flame can go.

It is an inevitable part of the evolution of any religious group that a certain mythology grows up around its founders; such figures are inspirational to their followers and pivotal in the history of the organizations they create, and so stories about them naturally tend to take on a life of their own. As these mythologies grow, it usually happens that after as little as one or two centuries have passed, it is no longer possible to say for sure what really happened at the beginning. That is one reason I have felt drawn to the Nichiren Buddhism of the Soka Gakkai. As a modern religion, the foundational events of which have occurred within my lifetime, or only slightly before, the Soka Gakkai offers an unparalleled opportunity to witness a new tradition in the process of being born.

From that point of view, what seems most striking to me about the first encounter between Josei Toda and the nineteen-year-old Daisaku Ikeda is the fact that it took place right at the borderline between the old religious paradigm and the new. As different as Makiguchi and Toda might have been in temperament, both had come of age in prewar Japan. Makiguchi could write about the importance of homeland in 1903, and even speak with affection about the Emperor system as a distinctly Japanese cultural form. And Toda, for all his gritty realism, had not foreseen the persecutions that befell the Soka Gakkai during World War II. Makiguchi's eyes were opened by the events that followed, and Toda's whole vision of life and Buddhism was permanently altered thereby. Both were pivotal figures whose ideas influenced modern Japanese society. But both men stood with one foot in the old world and one in the new.

By contrast, Daisaku Ikeda was born with both feet in the world we live in now. There is no ambiguity in his character, no yearning to preserve the traditional aspects of Japanese culture or religion. He is a man of postmodern tastes and sensibility, and I believe this must already have been apparent, probably even to Toda, when Ikeda was only nineteen years of age.

On the night he met Toda, Ikeda had been invited by some friends to what he probably thought was some kind of Cooperation and Friendship Group meeting to discuss the ideas of the French philosopher Henri Bergson. The confusion seems to have come from the title of Toda's lecture series, "A Philosophy of Life." Since Ikeda knew that Bergson had written a book by that same title, he naturally assumed that this was the subject of the meeting and agreed to attend and bring along two of his more serious-minded friends. The Soka Gakkai members who had issued the invitation knew, of course, that the subject was really Nichiren Buddhism but didn't know how to correct Ikeda's misperception without dampening his enthusiasm, and so they let the matter stand.

When Ikeda showed up at his first Soka Gakkai meeting on the night of August 14, he discovered that, although the subject seemed to be some kind of Buddhism, it was unlike any religious meeting he had ever heard of. There was no sermon or formal lecture. Rather, it seemed to be a discussion group like those frequented by so many Tokyo young people looking for answers (and mostly not finding them) during those early postwar years. Members asked questions, issued challenges, and—in general—seemed free to express themselves in a way that most would have found profoundly out of place, or even distasteful, in an ordinary religious setting, where formality and respect for authority are the rule. And yet the subject *was* religion, and as Ikeda listened, Toda made good on the promise to outline a coherent religious philosophy of life.

Discussion meetings such as the ones Ikeda had attended had been a feature of Tokyo society before wartime authorities restricted the freedom of speech, and so that aspect of the Soka Gakkai tradition was not, strictly speaking, an innovation. What *was* new was the pairing of religious worship with a format that allowed for free and open-minded inquiry, one that required participants to show actual proof in their lives of the teachings they were discussing. Such a thing had never existed before in Japanese religious culture. The closest equivalent was the *ko* system developed by Rennyo Shonin in the fifteenth century to spread the teachings of the Jodo Shinshu (the True Pure Land Buddhist sect). But the discussion groups initiated by Rennyo, although they were religious in nature, lacked a focus on the health and happiness of each individual. It is unlikely that those who attended them would have felt within their rights, for instance, to demand that the Jodo Shinshu teachings show practical application in daily life. In fact, the prohibition against intercessory prayer in Rennyo's tradition would actually have argued against it. By comparison, Toda's discussion meetings, a tradition inherited from Makiguchi and augmented by his reinterpretation of the Buddha as life force, were not only unprecedented, they were completely revolutionary. In the blending of religious teaching with freedom of expression and a firm practical resolve, such meetings carried the implicit promise of a completely new kind of religious experience. It was a promise they tended to keep.

This was the kind of meeting that Daisaku Ikeda—a man interested in finding a life philosophy but not necessarily a religion—had wandered into that night. He was young, thoughtful, and somewhat cosmopolitan in the way that big city-dwellers with access to many bookshops are the world over—though, of course, like everyone else in those days, he was poor. As a child of the war years, his very presence was a kind of challenge. "Give me something to believe in," it said, "some way of life that is truly workable, that gives a sustainable meaning to human existence, one that does not degenerate into poverty, disease, and war." Ikeda didn't need to speak those words aloud. They were understood. Young people were looking for answers, and the traditional repositories for such answers—politics, religion, and other cultural traditions—were empty or all but silent.

That night's discussion centered, appropriately enough, on a treatise on bringing peace to the land written by Nichiren in 1260. But eventually the subject came round to patriotism—a topic of great importance during the war years and great befuddlement later on, when Japan lay in ruins. Toda spoke in a way that neither Ikeda nor anyone else at the meeting had ever heard before. Real patriotism was *spiritual* patriotism, he insisted—the kind of patriotism that led one to *oppose* a war rather than join it.

Ikeda was impressed with Toda's insights and felt that, at last, he had found someone he could look up to, someone who seemed sure of himself and therefore wasn't put off by the kinds of questions that young people in those days urgently needed to ask. He left the meeting saying that he needed time to reflect on what he had heard—and time also to read about Buddhism, a subject he knew little about. Ten days later he joined the movement.

This is the version of the events found in Daisaku Ikeda's multi-volume historical novel *The Human Revolution*. As such, it represents a dramatized retelling of his first meeting with his lifelong mentor, Josei Toda. That doesn't mean, of course, that it isn't true. Ikeda's masterwork is intended to make the story of the Soka Gakkai accessible for the average person who finds it difficult to extract a coherent theme and story line from raw history. *The Human Revolution* provided something essential to the new movement, without which it probably could not have grown to the size it has. Those who criticize the novel as Ikeda's "revisionist history" of the Soka Gakkai have simply failed to understand what it is—which is a "gospel." *The Human Revolution's* thematically unified, story-like retelling of the events of the Soka Gakkai's founding allows members to embrace its message and spiritual lineage as their own. Just as it is difficult to imagine Christianity without the four gospels, it will be impossible for future generations to imagine the Soka Gakkai apart from the story line preserved in this mammoth work and its serialized sequel, *The New Human Revolution.*

And yet, Ikeda's fictionalized retelling of his own conversion leaves out . . . *the conversion itself!* He doesn't tell us what he thought about or explain how a single public meeting with a man he had never met before utterly changed the course of his life. Ten days later, he visited a Nichiren Buddhist temple and received the Gohonzon scroll, the sacred "object of devotion" inscribed by Nichiren that followers enshrine in their homes and chant Nam-myoho-renge-kyo to each morning and evening. About the conversion itself, he says almost nothing at all.

I was stunned when I first realized this, until I remembered that Ikeda had kept a private journal during those years. At very beginning of his book *A Youthful Diary: One Man's Journey From the Beginning of Faith to Worldwide Leadership for Peace,* Ikeda offers a brief but telling recollection of his first encounter with Toda:

> I remember being deeply impressed by the fact that, though imprisoned during the war by government authorities because of his reli-

gious beliefs, he had adamantly refused to give
in to the pressures brought to bear on him.

In the very next sentence he writes, "Some ten days later
I expressed a desire to join the Soka Gakkai."

What is striking about the experience Ikeda reports
in *A Youthful Diary*, brief as it is, is that it is virtually identical to the experience reported by Murata during the
"Kansai Campaign" of 1953 (which the three other Kansai veterans I met likewise all confirmed). And this, in
turn, was identical to the experience I had when I saw
Josei Toda's bottle cap prayer beads for the first time in
2003 and read about his resistance to the war. That I
did not convert to the Soka Gakkai but resolved to raise
awareness about the movement and its place in world
religion is itself a testament to Human Revolution—that
its teachings can inspire even those from other spiritual
traditions, bringing the world one step closer to the day
when all peoples can live on the same planet in peace.
Because if religion doesn't stand for peace, what *does* it
stand for? If one wanted to "wake the Buddha," that was
always the first question to ask. A religion that stood for
something *other* than peace couldn't meet the demands
of the twenty-first century. A religion that stood for something *other* than peace was simply fast asleep.

the culture of mentorship

FROM THE BEGINNING, one of the most remarkable things about the Soka Gakkai has been the close relationship between mentor and disciple. In itself this is not at all unusual. Buddhism has tended to focus on such relationships throughout its history, defining its various schools and sects according to the lineages by which they have been handed down. What is unique about the mentor-disciple relationship in the Soka Gakkai is the way it functions to empower members at every level of the organization, instead of just at the top.

Why does the Soka Gakkai have such a "mentorship culture," and what does that kind of culture mean? Like many simple questions, these have profound answers.

It is a natural human tendency once a tradition has been firmly set in place not to question how it came to be. Even when it functions well, there is a tendency to take it for granted. And so, to begin with, it is worth asking what the Soka Gakkai would look like *without* such relationships.

Suppose, for instance, that Tsunesaburo Makiguchi

had had a number of associates in developing the Soka
Gakkai but that none of these had followed him to
prison. Suppose further that, following the war, several
of these followers who had managed to avoid persecution decided to revive the organization. They would have
no choice but to build upon the principles of value-
creating education outlined in Makiguchi's writings
(those aspects of Makiguchi's thought and character
that could be grasped apart from a long-term commitment to the man himself).

Following that alternative history, it is always possible
that the organization could have instituted some kind
of educational reform in postwar Japanese society. However, it is unlikely that this would have gone through the
necessary phases of development to become a dynamic
international movement. Even if it had done so, it is
doubtful that such a movement could have become any
more influential than the one founded by Makiguchi's
Italian contemporary Maria Montessori. The Montessori
Method thrives today in a number of countries around
the world—especially in the United States, where
there are currently around eight thousand Montessori
schools—and few would dismiss its contributions to the
educational community. Nevertheless, it remains today
what it was when Montessori developed it: an alternative
to mainstream education practiced by relatively few.

When we think of it this way, the question is easy to

answer. Why did the Soka Gakkai develop its tradition of close mentor-disciple relationships? Because in the absence of such relationships (and the feelings of responsibility and gratitude they engender), there would be little apart from pure ideological ambition to motivate its growth and development. The movement would then have become driven by ideology instead of by people. Returning to our earlier analogy, it is not possible to light another person's candle unless you are standing close enough to do so. For lighting one candle with another is not the same as seeing another's lit candle from a distance and deciding to light a candle of one's own. In such cases there is no companionship, no community, no continuity—and no obligation to protect what, after all, is only the product of our own effort. When Daisaku Ikeda says that the oneness of mentor and disciple is the lifeblood of the Soka Gakkai, it is surely this living flame he is thinking of. Without it, the Soka Gakkai could not have become what it is today, nor would it hold much promise for the future. *TIME* magazine once described the Soka Gakkai as "an international people-to-people crusade against war." They were right about that much. People to people was exactly how Human Revolution spread.

In 2007, while working on an earlier Japanese version of *Waking the Buddha,* I was granted unprecedented access to virtually every top leader in the SGI. My conversations with these leaders were among the most interesting of my career as a religion writer. I should confess, however, that in each of those conversations, my primary objective wasn't to gather facts, anecdotes, and other kinds of information such as writers usually look for in crafting an article or a book. Nor was I hoping to form some general overall impression, arriving at a sense of the individual character of each man. My primary objective was, through dialogue, to compare the living flame of my own conversion (post-tribal, but not necessarily Nichiren Buddhist) with the flame that each of these men carried within him—flames which had been lit, as I later came to realize, through close personal contact with Daisaku Ikeda.

I wanted to determine whether that flame could act as I knew it must if it was to effect a worldwide spiritual revolution. Could it fulfill its promise to break free of the old paradigm? Or in the next generation would it fall back, by sheer force of gravity, into the older, drowsier model of Buddhism that stressed preserving privilege, ideological purity, and group identity above all else? And if it really *was* a new paradigm, what was the driving force behind it? What aspects of SGI culture would other religious groups around the world have to imitate or develop on their own if they wanted to move forward as the SGI had done? These were the questions at the forefront of my mind in virtually every conversation I had.

Every Soka Gakkai leader I interviewed spoke to me at one time or another about the central role of the mentor-disciple relationship in the life of the SGI, and several shared meaningful encounters of their own with Ikeda. One of the most memorable was a story told by Minoru Harada, president of the Soka Gakkai in Japan, about Ikeda's first trip to China in 1974 at the very height of the Cold War. I had heard much about the trip itself and its ultimate importance in normalizing Sino-Japanese diplomatic relations and slowing the nuclear build-up between China and the Soviet Union. But Harada's story did much to explain *why* the trip had been so successful.

As preparations were under way for the journey, Harada, who was chief secretary of the delegation, and his staff were busy with preparations, consulting books, guides, policy papers, newspaper clippings, and reports compiled by experts on Chinese history and culture—anything that they thought might increase their chances of a successful visit with Premier Zhou Enlai. At one point, when the conference table where they were meeting was completely covered with such materials and they were in the process of reading through the entire pile from top to bottom, Ikeda arrived for a visit. According to Harada, he took one look at the room and remarked,

"This is exactly what I was afraid of—this sort of thing will do you absolutely no good at all." Then, stepping forward to the table, he swept all the materials onto the floor. "What matters now is to go to China and observe things as they actually are and to report what you have seen."

Indeed, on that journey Ikeda made a simple but profound observation one day when he visited a Beijing elementary school and noticed the entrance to some kind of underground facility in the garden just behind the school. When he asked what was the purpose of this structure, he was told that it was a shelter for the children in case of nuclear attack. Later, he was shown the entrance to another shelter in the basement of a large department store in downtown Beijing, this one capable of housing the population of a small city. Were the people of Beijing afraid that a nuclear attack was imminent? he asked. He was told that, while they did not believe the leaders of their own country would begin a nuclear war (a fact later confirmed in Ikeda's conversations with China's leadership), they were terrified that Soviet leaders would.

There had been so much posturing between the leaders of the three major nuclear powers during the arms race, so much sword rattling and false bravado, that leaders on all sides had lost touch with the basic human feelings of their people. It is therefore all the more remarkable that, when Ikeda subsequently visited Soviet Premier Aleksei Kosygin three months later, he went armed only with this single direct observation: The Chinese people were profoundly afraid of the Soviet Union. He told Kosygin exactly what he had observed on that very immediate, very human level—that the Chinese were afraid, even their children—and were ready to defend themselves, but that they had no intention of attacking the Soviet Union first. He asked Kosygin what the Soviet Union's intentions were and was told that, like China, Russia would defend itself, but that its people would not begin a war.

Ikeda then confessed that the Japanese people were also deeply afraid of the Soviet Union and suggested that so much fear was bad for the people of Japan, China, and the Soviet Union. What good could the future hold for the Soviet Union if it inspired such profound fear in its neighbors? He asked Kosygin for permission to tell the Chinese leadership what had transpired at their meeting in order to decrease the level of fear all around, and Kosygin gave his consent. And, in what has to be one of the most daring acts of Cold War diplomacy ever conducted by a private individual, Ikeda did just that, relaying the message to Vice Premier Deng Xiaoping.

According to Harada, it was only years later that the

full impact of Ikeda's encounter with Kosygin came to light, as the historical record began to reflect that his meetings with Chinese and Soviet leaders had played an important role in stabilizing relations between the two countries. But all of this seems to have flowed directly from the power of face-to-face human contact. It was the theory of Human Revolution, practically applied in human relationships, that allowed Ikeda to accomplish what he did.

Years later, on one of his many trips to the Soviet Union, Ikeda met with Kosygin's oldest daughter. She told him that the late Soviet premier had returned home in a very uplifted mood the day he had met with the Soka Gakkai president. "I've just met a Japanese man who looked utterly ordinary," he told her. "But he turned out to be an extraordinary person after all. He was able to speak about extremely difficult issues in a way that made them plain and easy to understand."

Afterward, I reflected that, in my three-hour dialogue with Harada, not one Buddhist term or phrase was used. In fact, not once did I detect in his manner, his style of communication, or in what he said the kind of spiritual posturing I have come to expect in talking with religious leaders. Harada, and the message of peace and international goodwill that he obviously hoped to convey in our meeting, would have been at home anywhere in the world. In that, he proved a worthy disciple of the man Kosygin had described as being able to take extremely difficult issues and make them "plain and easy to understand."

the oneness of mentor
and disciple

O N AUGUST 14, 1952, exactly five years after his first
meeting with Josei Toda, Daisaku Ikeda arrived
in Osaka, at the heart of the Kansai region, having
been sent there as the youth leader to mount the Soka
Gakkai's first major outreach campaign outside of the
greater Tokyo area. "Let's rid Kansai of sickness and poverty," he said at the time. "In this faith there's no such
thing as impossible. When you base your life on prayer,
everything becomes possible."

It was a message people were waiting to hear. Of the
four Kansai veterans I met on my trip to the Soka Gakkai
center there, three had either been ill themselves when
they began their practice, or they were nursing a sick
family member. Akiko Kurihara, who began practicing
at twenty-one, told me that after the war her mother
was like a shattered teacup that had been glued back
together.

"She went to a Soka Gakkai meeting one day but
wasn't convinced to join," Kurihara told me. "My mother

had tried a number of different religions to see if they could cure her. But at the Soka Gakkai meeting they had refuted all the things she had tried, and she was in a very agitated state because of this. I asked her what they'd said, and she repeated it all to me. And I said: 'You know, I think they're right. It makes perfect sense to me.' And so I made my own determination on the spot and convinced my father to join, and then the three of us joined together. Strictly speaking, no one ever recruited me. The message that the Soka Gakkai had given my mother was such that, even hearing it secondhand, I knew it was right. After just one week, we went to a discussion meeting together."

Those were the days when the healing, life-centered message of the Soka Gakkai first went viral. Prior to Kansai, the movement had grown in a way that was impressive but nevertheless predictable, since it was due primarily to the persistence and hard work of its long-term members. Now the message traveled quickly, like fire spreading in a high wind. I was impressed when Masako Mineyama, who began practicing because she was sick and her family poor, first told me about Hisako Yayoi, a woman whose efforts to spread the Soka Gakkai message had become the stuff of local legend. But we all laughed a moment later when she explained that Yayoi had been practicing only ten days when she came over one afternoon to convert the Mineyama family because she knew they'd been struggling with illness. "I just joined myself and I'm not sure I understand it yet," Yayoi had explained, "but it seems like a great religion, and I really think you should join too."

Tadashi Murata recalls that when Ikeda first came to Kansai he was only twenty-four years old: "He was quite young, but he was so earnest and sincere, and so determined to make us healthy and happy, that you could feel it right away. In one of his letters Nichiren says, 'The purpose of the appearance in this world of Shakyamuni lies in his behavior as a human being.' President Ikeda demonstrated the truth of this through his own behavior. He told us that the Soka Gakkai was creating a religious revolution that would allow all humanity to become happy. Human Revolution he called it. He instilled in us a deep confidence that such a revolution really was possible, and it was this confidence that allowed us to change our lives. It was he who taught us the oneness of mentor and disciple."

"The oneness of mentor and disciple"—the expression grates on some people's ears. For some it calls to mind the cultish, uncritical veneration one sometimes sees for figures such as His Holiness the fourteenth Dalai Lama (who, admittedly, may be worthy of veneration) and such Indian gurus as Bhagwan Shree Rajneesh and Swami Rama, whose abuse of American followers led to numerous scandals and lawsuits.

Among the Japanese Soka Gakkai, however, the oneness of mentor and disciple is simply understood as the
necessary prerequisite for living a happy and productive
life. In a recent interview, Ikeda said something which,
I believe, highlights the difference between the oneness
of mentor and disciple as that tradition is understood
and handed down within the Soka Gakkai and the way
it is understood by those who see charismatic religious
leadership as primarily exploitive:

> In its early days, the Soka Gakkai was despised
> and laughed at in Japanese society as a gath-
> ering of the sick and poor. Josei Toda, my life
> mentor, took this as a point of pride, however,
> and declared with confidence: "The true mis-
> sion of religion is to bring relief to the sick and
> the poor. That is the purpose of Buddhism.
> The Soka Gakkai is the ally and friend of the
> common people, a friend to the unhappy.
> However much we may be looked down on,
> we will continue to fight for the sake of such
> people." Faced with the devastation of postwar
> Japan, Toda was convinced that, in the eyes of
> the Buddha, this was the most noble action.

I believe this explanation, although it makes no direct
reference to the mentor-disciple relationship, neverthe-

less explains perfectly how and why it works, and why it hasn't degenerated into mere guru-worship in the Soka Gakkai. That is because the relationship with a mentor in the Soka Gakkai tradition is fundamentally empowering and life-enhancing for the disciple. The Kansai pioneers I met, all of whom were directly mentored by Ikeda in the early days of the movement, spoke of him in terms of the utmost admiration and respect. And yet, at no point did their praise become a thing in itself. At no point was it disassociated from their own life-transformation. Their relationship with Ikeda was the subtext of recovery from serious illness. It was the back story of their journey back to solvency from financial ruin, the explanation for how, even in the face of great hardship, they had managed to rebuild the happiness of their families and their communities after the disappointments and deprivations of the war. The relationship was, in their minds, quite literally their ticket to a happy, healthy life. A story told by Setsuko Umemoto, who began practicing in July 1953, perfectly illustrates this point.

In 1956, when Daisaku Ikeda was traveling to Osaka each week to strengthen the organization there, the Soka Gakkai did not yet have a car at the Kansai Community Center. At the time, there was no alternative but to travel by train to the station in Wakayama, and go on from there to the meetings by bike.

Umemoto, who knew the area very well, was chosen to accompany Ikeda to five different meetings in a row, beginning with one meeting at 8:00 a.m. and stretching well into the evening. Between each meeting, they would have to hurry, biking up one hill after another. It was a grueling schedule and a long ride, Umemoto explained, but Ikeda had never complained. "We'd be going up and over lots of hills, and I'd say, 'Are you all right, Sensei?' And he'd say, 'Are *you* OK?' People were overjoyed to see him on these occasions, but I was the timekeeper, so I'd have to rush to move him along to the next place. There was never any time to rest. Finally, in the evening, there was the last meeting at Moto's place, but it was at the end of a very long hill. And finally Sensei would admit, 'I am so exhausted.'

"Sensei was completely frank and open at these meetings, and it was wonderful to see how relaxed everyone was with him. And even though he was exhausted at the end of the day, the members at the final meeting would always ask him for advice on a variety of personal issues, and so he would end up giving guidance well into the night. For me to have guided Sensei in this way was a very great honor. Everything I am today—every single thing I have been able to accomplish in my life—I feel it all goes back to those days."

spiritual independence

THERE ARE TWO EVENTS in the broader history of
the Soka Gakkai movement and the life of its third
president, Daisaku Ikeda, which are sure to be paired
together by future historians of the movement, even
though they took place more than fifteen years apart.
The first was the founding of the Soka Gakkai International on the island of Guam on January 26, 1975. The
second was the excommunication by Nichiren Shoshu
of the full combined membership of the Soka Gakkai
and the SGI on November 28, 1991, a date subsequently
referred to in Soka Gakkai lore as the "Day of Spiritual
Independence." Naturally, the first event is celebrated
annually by the SGI. But why the latter? Surely excommunication is nothing to be proud of.

When the Soka Gakkai was launched as a lay movement associated with Nichiren Shoshu, no one could
have predicted that it would grow to the size it did. Prior
to World War II, there was no history of any lay religious organization, in Japan or elsewhere, outgrowing
its sponsor organization to the extent that it virtually

dwarfed it, all but marginalizing the former religious ethos and replacing it with its own. There are doubtless many reasons why such a thing had never happened—cultural inertia, the sheer weight of priestly authority, and the difficulty (in Japan at least) of creating religious organizations independent of existing traditions. But, then, no one before Toda had ever offered an alternative to temple-based religious practice that could hold together—and even grow vigorously—in the absence of priestly direction.

As much as anything, it was neighborhood discussion meetings, held in members' homes, that accounted for the difference. The Soka Gakkai grew outward from hundreds, then thousands of such meeting places—and it grew very *quickly* from those nexus points, following the natural lines of human relationships. Members spoke to their neighbors about Nichiren Buddhism, or to their coworkers, or to their friends or extended families, and nothing was more natural than asking such people to attend a meeting at their home or at the home of a friend. It was utterly unlike being invited to attend a service or a lecture at a temple. True, the Soka Gakkai had a compelling message of optimism and hope—moreover, one that had "gone viral" in the early '50s and was therefore capable of leaping quickly across traditional boundaries. But without a post-tribal delivery system to match that viral message, the movement could not have grown as it did. Having to funnel the whole thing through a priest or a temple would have clogged the flow of the movement until it slowed to a trickle and finally came to a stop.

But it didn't. And once it became clear that the Soka Gakkai's vision for Buddhism would outgrow the Japanese religious sensibility of its Nichiren Shoshu sponsors, it was just a matter of time before the Soka Gakkai International was born.

The third and final phase in the development of the Soka Gakkai—the phase of completion—could not have taken place without the internationalization of the movement, which began formally with the creation of the SGI on Guam in 1975, and informally in 1960, with Ikeda's first trip to America. Follow a linear history of the movement, and it is easy to see how the Soka Gakkai began as an educator's association in and around Tokyo; how it then developed into a stable organization with a unified, compelling religious message and a large, influential membership throughout Japan; and finally how it spread quickly around the globe. But I don't believe that linear approach to the Soka Gakkai's history can account for the size, strength, and diversity of the organization we see today. The potential for the Soka Gakkai to become a global movement was implicit from the very beginning, in much the same way that the plan for an entire oak—or even a *forest* of oaks—is there inside of the acorn from the moment it first strikes the ground.

Already, in the discussion group model formulated by Tsunesaburo Makiguchi, there was a post-tribal agenda at work. Whether he intended it or not, the combining of a discussion format with religious worship could have led nowhere else. It was a decisive step outside the older religious paradigm, which tended to center upon temple affiliation. In the absence of priestly oversight, it was only a matter of time before the people meeting in such groups would begin to develop goals and ideas of their own. Likewise, it was also only a matter of time before they came to reinterpret such core Nichiren Buddhist teachings as "Bodhisattvas of the Earth" and "the Buddha as an ordinary human being" in terms of their own self-empowerment as lay people. Absent the priestly, temple-centered religious culture, it was natural that the Soka Gakkai's approach to converting others to the faith would become less ideologically driven over time. Perhaps Toda had anticipated this when he posed his challenge to the young Ikeda: "It is a vast world. There are many peoples, many races. . . . We'll have to start thinking about how to disseminate the Mystic Law in such places." But even to Toda it was probably not clear how powerful a shaping force that global destiny was to become in the future of the SGI.

The SGI stretched the old priestly religious paradigm

to the point of breaking. Like Jesus's "old wineskins," that priestly model could not contain a global mission like that of the SGI. In his final days, Toda seems to have intuited all of this. His last conversations with Ikeda focused on two seemingly unrelated matters: the globalization of the movement's outreach efforts and the need for the Soka Gakkai to oppose corruption within the Nichiren Shoshu priesthood. In *The Human Revolution*, Ikeda records Toda's "final injunction" to him: "You must fight adamantly against any evil that takes root within the priesthood. . . . You must never retreat a single step. Never slacken in your struggle against such evil."

With the benefit of fifty years' hindsight, I think it is possible to see in Toda's final directives to his young disciple a concern not simply with priestly corruption in its more ordinary guises like pride or greed—to which the Nichiren Shoshu priesthood is surely no more susceptible than the Catholic hierarchy or other groups where money and property are involved—but rather that such corruption would somehow impede the spread of Buddhism. It's not clear that Toda connected the two issues directly in his mind, but the fact that he was thinking so urgently about these matters at the end of his life suggests that, on some level at least, he foresaw that the Soka Gakkai would need its autonomy from the priestly tradition in order to continue on the trajectory he had established for it. In that case, the real evils Toda was referring to were those conservative religious impulses that might try to bring Human Revolution down to the scale of traditional piety or ritual observance, rather than allowing it to develop into the kind of full-blown Buddhist humanism that could transcend barriers of race, religion, or creed.

It was always unrealistic to expect that a conservative religious institution like Nichiren Shoshu would be able to keep pace with an empowered lay movement that was more than willing to sacrifice Japanese cultural attitudes and customs for the sake of spreading Buddhism around the globe. From the beginning, Toda saw priestly authority as purely supplemental to that freer, more dynamic style of outreach. The founding of the Soka Gakkai International in 1975 by his successor, Daisaku Ikeda, was therefore right in line with the trajectory of the movement. But creation of the SGI virtually guaranteed its ultimate excommunication by Nichiren Shoshu. In a perfect world, such a painful and acrimonious split would not have been necessary. But, then, in a perfect world the priests themselves would have realized the limits of their own authority. That the priesthood was unwilling or unable to do so says much about the degenerative effects of religious authoritarianism and privilege. But mostly it shows that the old religious model was in deep decline. That decline was itself an invitation to the populist, egalitarian reforms of the Soka Gakkai.

The logic for such reforms had, after all, already been suggested by the Lotus Sutra. It only remained for these latter day bodhisattvas to light a candle from the flame on the altar, then carry it outside of the temple where it could spread freely to the many peoples of the world.

even to the fiftieth person

O N   T H E   T A B L E next to my bed, along with texts like the Bible, the Qur'an, the Bhagavad-Gita, and *The Writings of Nichiren Daishonin*, there is a pale purple paperback I have consulted so frequently over the past several years that it is now almost falling apart. This is volume four of *The Wisdom of the Lotus Sutra*.

Because I have read the passage so many times, the book often falls opens to the lines I highlighted in red ink on the day I bought it in 2003. They were the first words of teaching I ever saw from Daisaku Ikeda:

> When we realize that our lives are one with the great and eternal life of the universe, we are the Buddha. The purpose of Buddhism is to enable all people to come to this realization.

I understood those words the first time I read them and even had a sense that they represented a shift in the way people might begin to think about religion, but it was only during a conversation with Soka Gakkai General

Director Masaaki Masaki that I began to grasp the model they described.

Masaki recalled that after the break with the Nichiren Shoshu priesthood in 1991, he was inspired to reflect more deeply on the history of Buddhism and its various reform movements. It was a mistake to suppose that there was only one Lotus Sutra, he told me. President Toda had taught that there were at least three versions of the sutra already: the Lotus Sutra of Shakyamuni, the Lotus Sutra of T'ien-t'ai, and the Lotus Sutra of Nichiren.

"The essence of the various Lotus Sutras is, of course, the same," he explained. "But the way in which the sutra needs to be presented depends on the conditions of the age and the capacity of the people who read it. Shakyamuni taught the four noble truths and the eight-fold path. Later, the Chinese sage T'ien-t'ai explained the ever-present nature of all reality in terms of 'three thousand realms in a single moment of life.' And still later, Nichiren taught Nam-myoho-renge-kyo. My own feeling is that there is a contemporary expression of the Lotus Sutra based on these and that this is what the three presidents of the Soka Gakkai have appeared in the world to teach. They have an obligation to teach the same essence as the other three sutras, of course, but in accordance with modes of expression that are appropriate to this age."

Masaki asked if I agreed that it was legitimate to adapt the teachings in this way, and I replied by quoting the opening line of one of Nichiren's most famous treatises: "When it comes to studying the teachings of Buddhism, one must first learn to understand the time." Masaki explained that President Toda had taken the essence of these earlier teachings and revealed them in the doctrine that "the Buddha is life itself." This was the core message of the Soka Gakkai and the essence of its approach to the Lotus Sutra. "All these point to the same thing—the same reality that is common to all," he said. "Through his emphasis on the path of mentor and disciple, President Ikeda is teaching us how to put that new Lotus Sutra into practice."

I told him that, based on my study of the Soka Gakkai and its teachings, I believed that it was not merely Shakyamuni Buddha who was "always in the world," as the sixteenth chapter of the Lotus Sutra taught, but the Lotus Sutra itself. It was the nature of that sutra to remain always *alive* in the world; therefore, it found a way to get taught in each new epoch. I suggested it was possible to establish a kind of test to prove the appearance of a new sutra, not so much in terms of what it said as what it *did*.

When a new Lotus Sutra was born, that recalibrated message was so perfectly suited to the time and to the needs of the people that it could travel "up to the fiftieth person," as the sutra had predicted, and still retain its message. In other words, the revolutionary flame of that message would tend to pass very quickly from person to person without losing any of its force and effect, "waking the Buddha" inherent in each individual as it traveled from hand to hand and heart to heart. As centuries passed, however, inevitably such a message would come to be understood by fewer and fewer people, until at last it could travel to only one other person. At that point a new version would be born in order to preserve its message. The way we know that a new Lotus Sutra has been born is that, suddenly, it can travel fifty people deep again. And the way I knew that a new expression of the Lotus Sutra has been born during the latter part of the twentieth century was that its message had spread in this way, reaching deep into the societies where it had traveled. This I had seen with my own eyes. The spirit of Human Revolution as taught by Daisaku Ikeda—empowering individuals and the championing of common human values—could be communicated to anyone, anywhere across the globe. How? Simply by telling them that what mattered was the dignity and value of their own lives—that if they could affirm that value and that dignity, the message would spread . . . and the world would change around them.

I had many opportunities to speak with the Soka Gak-kai leadership about this "new sutra" on my visits to Japan, including the late Soka Gakkai Study Department Chief Katsuji Saito. The most significant part of our conversation involved Ikeda's teachings on religious humanism. As Saito explained: "Buddhism is a humanistic religion, and the Soka Gakkai is the form of Buddhism that most clearly expresses Buddhism's humanistic aspect. The basic stance of Buddhism, from a humanistic point of view, is that an ordinary human being can become a Buddha. Ikeda has consistently stressed that Buddhism exists for the sake of ordinary human beings and that the mission of the Soka Gakkai is to clarify that fact and bring it to the fore."

Expressed so simply, this hardly seems like a revolutionary idea. In fact, as used in general conversation, the term *humanism* has become so vague and bland that it is hard to say exactly what it refers to. For this reason, in the West, humanism has become an exceptionally weak philosophical position, roughly analogous to the term *secular*, with which it is often paired. Today it has come to refer to a philosophical position that finds value in human life, human knowledge, and human society, irrespective of any religious system of value or belief. To say that one is a "secular humanist" in America is invariably to designate oneself an atheist, though perhaps an optimistic one.

There is no well-established tradition of religious

humanism in the West. God may have created human beings in His image, according to the Bible, but we Westerners tend not to believe that we can trust in that belief to the extent of building a religion on being human. Perhaps this is due to the Christian idea of humanity as "fallen," or perhaps it is the result of the rift between Greco-Roman rationalism and Jewish monotheism, which sent science and philosophy off packing in one direction and religion in another. But even in the relatively timeless writings of Marcus Aurelius we find the split deeply pronounced, as if it had been there from the beginning. "Either Providence or Atoms!" he proclaims. Either there is God ordering all things for the best, or there is humanity, struggling nobly, but somewhat blindly against the backdrop of a beautiful but indifferent universe.

This was precisely the value of Human Revolution for the West, I suggested to Saito. In the Lotus-based teachings of the Soka Gakkai we find an approach to humanism that, at last, is vigorous enough to stand alongside religion as an equal partner in conferring dignity, meaning, and value on human life. To articulate this position—and to *strengthen* it—has been the primary purpose of Daisaku Ikeda's landmark dialogues with philosophers, statesmen, and scientists from around the world. With his mentor-driven practice of raising up each individual as the basis for Human Revolution,

Ikeda has internationalized a message that seems destined to become universal over the coming century, as it spreads to other religions, other cultures, and other ways of thought. The SGI has a very special mission in spreading that new religious model around the world.

the ultimate declaration

THIS BRINGS US to a question that often generates some controversy, both in the United States and Japan—namely, how much is the Soka Gakkai driven by its religious humanism and how much by the personality of its third president, Daisaku Ikeda? "Ikedaism" his detractors sometimes call it, claiming that the SGI president demands unquestioning loyalty of his followers, insinuates himself into international affairs through various dialogues and peace declarations, and curries favor with foreign colleges, institutes, and universities—institutions which subsequently add to his growing list of honorary degrees. Almost no one I met within the SGI voiced agreement with such criticisms. Nevertheless, new members sometimes struggle to understand the near-ubiquitous presence of Daisaku Ikeda in the Soka Gakkai as its third and sole living founder. His photo is everywhere. And the other members speak of him in terms of utmost respect and veneration, like a trusted guide or a beloved teacher. They refer to him as "my mentor," although few had ever had any direct contact with the man. At some point in the early decades of the twenty-first century, Ikeda will pass away and the problem (if there really is one) will cease to exist. It is the nature of religious founders to command this kind of veneration from the people whose lives they have changed. But societies seem to have an easier time accepting them once they're dead.

Because I have spent so much time in dialogue with the Soka Gakkai, both in the United States and Japan, I've been accorded a kind of honorary status in the movement, even though I am not myself a practicing Nichiren Buddhist. That is why, when I travel on business, I sometimes attend meetings in various places. There's something inspiring about the fact that, almost anywhere in America today, I can find a discussion meeting to go to. After one or two phone calls I can simply show up unannounced for an evening of chanting and discussion.

That was how I came to catch a ride back to my hotel one night with an SGI-USA member I had never met before. She had been exposed to the movement some years earlier but had decided to join only the year before. She had many friends already in the SGI and regularly attended discussion meetings and other activities, she told me. She'd recently even undertaken to tell others about the faith. But there was a problem. "What do you honestly think about Daisaku Ikeda?" she asked me finally as we were pulling up to the hotel, "because the truth is

I'm a little bothered by all the adoration he receives—and all those honorary degrees! I just don't know what to think about all that. Sometimes I feel like I'm not a real member of the organization because I can't get behind that kind of hero worship. What should I do?"

I explained that I was not an authority on the SGI but only a person who was intensely curious about it. I had done the SGI's chanting practice very rigorously for some time in order to understand it more fully, trying to grasp its teachings from within the movement rather than judging them from a safe objective distance as most scholars and journalists chose to do. But I was not a believer in the same way that those who attended the meeting with us had been. She should speak to one of them about her concerns. I didn't know if she'd be convinced by what they said about Ikeda and his role in their lives, but at least she would be getting her answer from a person who had experienced the mentor-disciple relationship from within the organization and could therefore testify to its effect on their lives.

But she would not be deterred.

"I want to hear what *you* think," she said firmly. "I really do."

A few weeks before this encounter, the SGI had celebrated the seventeenth anniversary of its excommunication by Nichiren Shoshu—the day which, in a sense, marked its birth as a new religious paradigm.

"If November 28, 1991, is the SGI's Spiritual Independence Day," I asked her, "then what would you call the SGI Gohonzon, the scroll it distributes to its members, which they house in their altar cabinet and chant to every day?"

She looked puzzled at first, but after a moment she smiled. "I guess you could call it our Declaration of Independence."

"And whose signature first comes to mind when you visualize the Declaration of Independence?" I asked.

Here her face clouded over. I knew that I had confirmed her worst suspicions.

"John Hancock's," she answered, with evident distaste.

Like most Americans, all she knew of John Hancock was that he had written his name in ostentatiously large script when he signed the Declaration, so that it loomed large on the document, much bigger than the signatures of the other signers. That is why people sometimes say "just put your John Hancock here" when requesting a signature for a petition or a legal document. The name is synonymous with an unusually big ego, and I could tell that, initially at least, I had confirmed her worst fears about Ikeda. But I wasn't finished yet.

A legend grew up around Hancock that he had signed his name in large script "so that England's king could read it without his spectacles," I told her. It was, in other words, a brave and audacious gesture, mixed with more than a little bravado. However, this story was almost certainly apocryphal, since it didn't appear in the historical record until many years later. The real story was far more impressive.

The document we have today is not the original Declaration of Independence. The document sent to the printer has been lost and may even have been destroyed in the printing process. What we do have is the famous "Dunlap broadside," the first published version of the Declaration that was widely distributed throughout the American colonies and would therefore have been visible to everyone, including the British Army. The first version of that treasonous document, the only Declaration available for the first six months, included the printed name of only one signer: John Hancock, president of the Continental Congress. The other names were added later to the handwritten version that resides today in the National Archive. One theory as to why Hancock's signature looms so large on that later document is that it was meant to recognize the special risk he took. Being the first signer, in the event the Revolution was a failure, he would logically also have been the first to be hung.

"And who was the first signer of the Gohonzon?" I asked.

"Nichiren," she answered.

I told her to go home that night and look very carefully at Nichiren's name inscribed vertically right below the characters for Nam-myoho-renge-kyo. "Notice how large and bold it is," I told her. "And think about what that might mean."

"Nichiren risked his life every step of the way in order to spread his teachings on the Lotus Sutra, beginning with the first time he publicly declared Nam-myoho-renge-kyo as the ideal teaching for people living in an era of struggle and strife. 'On Establishing the Correct Teaching for the Peace of the Land,' the letter of protest he wrote to the military government, was one of his declarations, signed by no one but himself. And after that there were many others. Finally, he inscribed the Gohonzon, also signed by no one but himself, and wrote his name larger than ever before. It was his ultimate declaration, undertaken with the ultimate risk.

"When you see Daisaku Ikeda's name 'written large' within the organization," I told her, "or on his honorary degrees, or when you see him participating in public forums like dialogues with famous intellectuals or world leaders, you should realize that he is also signing all these with his life force and his lifeblood, just as Tsunesaburo Makiguchi did when he wrote articles critical of the Imperial government, and as Josei Toda did when he delivered his declaration for the abolition of nuclear weapons. After that you can ask yourself a simple question: When the opportunity comes to add your own name to the roster for Human Revolution—through practice, through spreading the teachings, through goodwill to all other peoples throughout the world—will you hesitate to add your name to that declaration? And if not, *why* not? Isn't it because of the examples you have seen— examples of honor, like Tsunesaburo Makiguchi, who died rather than betray his beliefs; of compassion, like Josei Toda, who championed the causes of the sick and the poor; and of fearless determination, like Daisaku Ikeda, who plunged ahead into the twenty-first century with a message for all humanity in every country around the globe?"

I told her that she still ought to seek the advice of others within the movement. Nevertheless, since she had pressed me for an answer, these were my honest thoughts on the figure of Daisaku Ikeda, third president of the Soka Gakkai and founder of the SGI.

the future

a religion for the twenty-first century

the foundation for a happy life

As the Soka Gakkai International continues to spread its paradigm-shifting message around the globe, two issues are central to the health and vitality of its mission: the mentor-disciple relationship and the passing down of Soka Gakkai tradition within families. The first explains how the Soka Gakkai's message has spread so far so quickly. The second explains how that message puts down roots as a permanent culture in the societies it has traveled to.

I recently met with a New York University professor who is a lead researcher in the newly emerging field of meditation-based neuroscience. We began by talking about the health benefits—mental and physical—experienced by practitioners of Buddhist meditation but ended up talking about the mentor-disciple relationship as it is experienced by Asian and American Buddhists.

An experienced practitioner in half a dozen different spiritual disciplines, most of them Buddhist, this researcher conducts studies investigating the effects of meditation on the brain. We had been friends for some years and had often discussed the Soka Gakkai but never in connection with his work. That night, as he described the results of one of his most recent investigations, I shared the story I told earlier in this book about the journalist who had tried to write an article on the life-changing effects of meditation practice, only to find that very few Western practitioners could cite specific ways in which their lives had changed as a result of their meditation.

He explained that the effects of meditation tended to include generalized feelings of well-being and greater mental clarity, in addition to a host of physiological health benefits, including lower blood pressure and enhanced resistance to stress and pathogens like viruses. He conceded, however, that meditators tended not to claim what Nichiren and the Soka Gakkai called "actual proof" of the teaching—specific instances when their practice had inspired them to make positive life changes or led them to confront and surmount a particular obstacle to happiness in their lives.

I suggested he might want to consider studying the effects of chanting Nam-myoho-renge-kyo on the brain. Meditation was an esoteric discipline practiced by relatively few people worldwide. Surely, if there were significant neurological and health benefits to Buddhist chanting (as I was sure there would be), these would make for a far more interesting set of scientific results than the studies now being conducted, if only because there were so many more people around the world chanting some kind of Buddhist mantra each day than there were meditating. He'd never considered the logic of this before and couldn't remember ever hearing anyone make such a suggestion. But that wasn't the most interesting part of our conversation.

Just as the discussion seemed to be winding down, he asked a question I had never considered before. "Really, what is the difference between chanting and meditation? And does that difference really account for the different experiences of American meditators and members of the SGI? Maybe there are also other factors involved."

At first I insisted that the dynamic experience of vocal sound and the vigor with which SGI members chanted accounted for their more active, hands-on approach to life. Meditation was relaxing—and it could certainly give rise to feelings of peace and contentment—but wasn't it for these very reasons less likely to leave you feeling determined or "fired up"? Wasn't it less likely to make you truly energized and "awake"? He pointed out that there were meditative practices in the Tibetan tradition that produced the same feelings, even though they often involved no audible chanting. Practitioners of tantric meditation employed visualization exercises that led to higher levels of energy, greater physical and emotional vitality, and the determination to break through obstacles. These were well known and now widely practiced throughout the world, even though they tended to be focused on abstract spiritual goals like fulfilling the obligations of a bodhisattva way of life, rather than on the practical challenges and difficulties of daily life. He wondered if there might be some other factor at work in producing the "actual proof" that Soka Gakkai members claimed. That was when the conversation took an unexpected turn and we began to talk about mentor and disciple.

As we compared notes about interviewing Asian and American Buddhists about their experiences of Buddhist practice, we discovered that we'd both noticed the same anomaly. Ask an American convert and an Asian Buddhist the same question about their practice, and you'd get two completely different kinds of answer.

The difference was this. A person raised in America would speak frankly and openly about their individual experience with Buddhism and the spiritual benefits they felt they had gained from it. Ask someone raised in Asia, and they would speak about their teacher—the spiritual mentor who had taught them the practice— and the benefits of their *relationship* with that person. If they had experienced significant gains or improvements in their life, these would be explained in the context of that relationship, as if the relationship itself had been what made these things happen.

In the minds of Asian Buddhists we had interviewed, there was no sense of their spiritual practice as a thing belonging to themselves alone. It was part of a transmission. Ask them a question about their practice, and invariably you got the *story* of that transmission. It made sense to American Buddhist converts to speak of their practice in highly personalized, individualistic terms as something they had done themselves and gained benefit from. To Asian Buddhists, it was not an isolated practice that had changed or inspired them—it was the person. The difference was profound.

I had experienced this again and again over the ten-year period when I interviewed SGI members about their practice. Non-Asian SGI-USA members were more likely than their Japanese counterparts to report their experiences in individualistic terms. Even so, they nearly always mentioned within the first minute or two the leadership, inspiration, and encouragement offered to them by Daisaku Ikeda or other SGI members who had helped or inspired them as a key factor in their experience. In Japan, a typical conversation would begin with words like, "I first heard Sensei speak when I was twenty-eight" or "Everything I have achieved in my life is due to my relationship with Sensei." Both SGI-USA members and their Japanese spiritual cousins had found in the mentor-disciple relationship a sense of personal connection and inspiration that had inspired them to seek happiness and fulfillment in their lives.

Admittedly, the mentor-disciple relationship is the most commonly misunderstood aspect of Soka Gakkai culture in the West today. Partly, this is due to the terminology involved. In English the term "mentor" is rarely used in spiritual settings, and "disciple" is used primarily to refer to the first twelve followers of Jesus. Christians may speak of "discipleship" as a religious ideal to aspire to, but they call themselves disciples at the risk of being thought spiritually presumptuous or psychologically unhinged. Applied to a living person, the word *disciple* usually has a secular meaning. It refers to a person whose devotion to a cause is so fervent it assumes an almost fanatical religious quality. Its religious uses are therefore often negative. Americans view discipleship as a psychologically perilous undertaking that may cost them their individuality and their will. Mentors are usually professors, business people, or artisans from whom there is something useful or practical to learn. Neither term means to the average American what it means to the SGI. Getting to know an SGI member or attending discussion meetings can eventually demonstrate for the average person the dynamic power of the mentor-disciple relationship, distinguishing it from, say, the guru-disciple relationship, which is usually much less centered on the life of the individual. But first he or she has to overcome an almost inborn cultural prejudice, reflected in our language itself, against the idea that the quality of a devotional relationship can be the determining factor in one's experience of success or failure in life.

As a people, Americans tend to be resourceful, individualistic, and self-reliant. Such virtues are commendable in themselves—a necessary aspect of the pioneer spirit that led our original settlers here. And yet, in embracing those very virtues we run the risk of isolating ourselves. Competition, which leads to greater economy, productivity, and efficiency in society at large, becomes a detriment to the individual when it keeps us from realizing that, as living beings, we stand or fall based on the quality of our relationship to others and to the world. Not one of us exists alone.

Though its wisdom is simple and universal, this principle has been the foundation of Buddhist teachings from its very earliest days. The Buddha taught a doctrine of interdependence and inclusivity that delivers suffering beings from loneliness and isolation, allowing them to build a life based on those positive, progressive values that are of benefit not only to the individual but to society at large. But that wisdom begins with a relationship, and the quality of that relationship determines whether we can attain such wisdom or not. If it is a relationship of mutual trust and devotion, that relationship becomes the foundation for a happy life. If it is built on suspicion or contempt, there is no basis for progress. There is no way out of suffering and loneliness. In which case life really *is* suffering, just as the Buddha taught—because then we live and die alone.

This is, I believe, the real message behind the mentor-disciple relationship now said to be the foundation of the Soka Gakkai and the heart of its message. On the one hand, that message consists of the one word *life* that Josei Toda saw flash before his mind's eye in prison during a moment of sudden illumination. It is likewise the message that Daisaku Ikeda has affirmed countless times, and in myriad ways, in his speeches, dialogues, and writings. But what is life if not an ever-widening circle of dynamic, interdependent relationships? And what will the *quality* of those relationships be without a model for them? That is the purpose of the mentor—to provide the model for life.

boomers, buddhism, and beyond

THE FAMILY IS the basic social unit in all human
societies. It has therefore long been the glue that
holds spiritual traditions together. No spiritual tradition
has ever survived in the absence of family. Even those
that did not directly support or condone family life—
celibate orders like Theravada Buddhism in South Asia
or Shakerism in America—were still dependent for their
continued survival on families who sponsored their practice financially or provided an influx of new members
with each passing generation. The life of the family is
intimately connected with religion—or should be. A religion that ignores the role of the family, or that offers
nothing of value for families, is not long for this world.

Several years ago I wrote an article that gained wide
attention in America, eventually making its way into the
Wall Street Journal and the *New York Times*. The article was
called "Dharma Family Values (Or, Why American Buddhism Must Change or Die)," and its premise was simple:
In America, Buddhism tended to be a solitary pursuit

rather than a family affair; therefore, its days were probably numbered. The current generation of "Boomer Buddhists" would die, leaving no lasting American Buddhist movement behind.

The problem was that fathers or mothers would go off on meditation retreats once or twice a year, or attend regular meetings at their local Zen center or Tibetan Buddhist temple, but they seldom took their children along. Few Buddhist centers in America had regularly scheduled activities for families. They didn't even have Buddhist holidays to build a family culture around, like Jews did with Passover and Christians with Easter and Christmas. Perhaps most significant of all, they tended not to offer christenings, weddings, or funerals. You could meditate as a Buddhist in America, and you could chant, drum, and in some places even beg for alms, but you couldn't get born or married. In many cases, you couldn't even die as a Buddhist. When it came to the kinds of observances that are sacred to families, Buddhism had little to offer.

The article generated a remarkable range of responses. Some American Buddhists were angry at me for what they regarded as an unjust attack. Others, mostly young Buddhists with families, wrote to thank me for pointing out the obvious flaw in the American Buddhist fabric. Years later, the article continues to get cited in newspapers and magazine articles about Buddhism, and the debate it started continues in American Buddhist centers and temples around the country.

In the year it appeared, there was only one American Buddhist group that responded enthusiastically to what I wrote in "Dharma Family Values," and that was the SGI-USA. Admittedly, I had praised the SGI for its efforts to include young people. The SGI met mostly in members' homes, had meetings for teens, and even very young children were often included in its activities. It hadn't evolved any yearly Buddhist holidays that I knew of (though the SGI had plenty of celebrations of its own), and I didn't think it had a formal ceremony in place for christenings, but on the whole they were doing better than most. Not only that, when the article came out, the SGI was the only organization to seek advice on how they might do more for families than they were already doing. They cared about families and about young people and wanted to be sure they felt included in the movement's activities.

This was the most hopeful sign for the future I had seen from any group, and it was about that time I began advising other American Buddhist organizations to study the SGI and imitate as many of its practices and policies as possible. As I wrote to a Buddhist teacher friend, "You don't have to agree with their teachings or adopt their style of practice, but you'd be a fool not to notice where they're succeeding and learn from it."

In Japan, where the Soka Gakkai originated, there is a long tradition of what might be called "Family Buddhism"—so long, in fact, that many now consider it an intractable problem. The term "Funeral Buddhism" has been used in recent years to describe institutions which, having outlived their use and therefore no longer relevant to life in a modern, secular state, are now only a shell of their former selves. Such institutions offer funerals and memorial services but little else, and these at exorbitant prices. Recently, some Japanese families have felt so financially abused by the Buddhist temples that their families have maintained an affiliation with, sometimes for many centuries, that they have gone so far as to hire freelance priests to say the services instead. These families believe that their temple priest has nothing real or legitimate to offer them, and so they simply pay for the service itself. Any priest will do. In such cases, the relationship that once existed between family and temple is itself in need of a funeral. It is now officially dead.

The vitality of the Soka Gakkai stands in stark contrast to the "Funeral Buddhism" so prevalent in Japan. Generations of Soka Gakkai members have now attended schools founded upon Makiguchi's theory of value-creating education, and Soka University now has graduates of its various institutions teaching in its halls, both in the United States and in Japan. As time goes on, perhaps these institutions will no longer be so closely identified with the Soka Gakkai as a religious institution, just as today, in America, a student can attend a four-year university without every learning that it was originally a religiously sponsored institution or that it maintains a religious affiliation today. For now, however, there remains a lively and inspired sense among the students at these institutions that their experience at home, at school, and in some cases even at work, are all coherently focused.

I would maintain that this cohesive kind of experience is possible because the Soka Gakkai has introduced a new paradigm—both in religion and in religiously inspired education—that embraces the full range of life enthusiasms. Within Soka Gakkai families, there are surely children who grow up and move on to other things, just as there are in all families. But this tends to happen more in families that have lost their spark, families that are so bound by tradition that the only way to experience freedom is to *break* with that tradition, renouncing some aspect of it, if for no other reason than to make room for something new. For now the Soka Gakkai *is* that new thing. In fact, the Soka Gakkai may well be the newest thing in the world.

In the end, it was that new thing that led me to study the Soka Gakkai International in depth and conduct dialogues with so many of its members. At the beginning of that study I posed myself a question: What does a religious movement like the SGI mean for the larger economy of religious cultures? What does the appearance of the SGI mean spiritually for the world at large?

facing the challenge ahead

SINCE WORLD WAR II, cultures across the planet have been in transition as humanity has tried to grapple for the first time in its history with truly global issues— species-wide challenges like overpopulation, diminishing water supplies, nuclear proliferation, and global climate change. Prior to the explosion in information technology, the contours of these problems were visible to few and clear to none. Now almost everybody sees them.

As a result, humanity finds itself faced with the necessity to move forward as a species and—with greater ease of building community through communication across the globe—it finally has the means to do so. Naturally, this means that we human beings will have to radically rethink the way we organize our activities as a species— the way we address our problems, and even the way we *think* about them. Instead of competing against one another as separate races, nationalities, or religions, effectively creating a world in which for some to prevail others must necessarily lose or be cast away, we will have to think of ourselves as a whole. We will have to find a new philosophy and a new language for expressing that wholeness, and new ways of grappling with the meaning and value of life itself.

If we accept this need, it becomes clear at once that a post-tribal, life-centered religious movement like the SGI—with its global mission to promote universal human values like peace, education, and culture—is right on time. In fact, the case could be made that it actually arrived a little early. Tsunesaburo Makiguchi had already felt its stirrings in 1903 and by 1944 was ready to die for it, even though what "it" was, apart from an educational organization with an egalitarian format for its meetings, wasn't yet fully clear. When Josei Toda left Toyotama Prison in 1945, he carried within him a thoroughly modern reinterpretation of the Lotus Sutra, and by the time of his death in 1958, his understanding of just how *big* that new interpretation was had developed to the point that he could imagine it spreading across the globe. More than that, he could foresee that Buddhism itself would have to evolve in order to embrace that wider mission and left a clear, compelling legacy of post-tribal declarations and recommendations on how to inspire that revolution during the last year of his life, both to the Soka Gakkai youth and to his disciple Daisaku Ikeda.

With the benefit of the head start provided by Tsunesaburo Makiguchi, the life-centered religious philosophy of Josei Toda, and the humanistic vision and international networking of Daisaku Ikeda, the Soka Gakkai has now spread to 192 countries across the globe with its message of Human Revolution. That fact more than any other suggests that it has taken the lead in spreading the new paradigm for religious practice, for there was no analogous twentieth-century religious movement in Judaism, Christianity, Hinduism, or Islam. In fact, as a spiritual movement, the Soka Gakkai offers a much broader and more versatile model than we normally see in a religious paradigm. Its egalitarian, international ethos, mixed with a home-based discussion group model and a focus on the human potential for altruism and peaceful cooperation are the basis for a "sustainable" model of progress. It's the next model because its focus remains on progress in culture, in human rights, and the human spirit, rather than on the ever-multiplying array of products that masquerades as progress, distracting us from our humanity and poisoning the Earth on which we live.

To the degree that we can at last come together as a species to realize the core values we share in common as human beings, we will learn to preserve and celebrate those values in the only way possible going forward—by finding sustainable ways of life and commerce that allow us to live in harmony, not just with one another, but with the planetary ecosystem itself. Does the SGI stand the best chance of "passing the flame" of those core human values across the planet? Honestly, I don't know. But I am increasingly certain that the SGI is the only *type* of religion that might be up to the job. And yet its job description is a sobering one. Because the SGI created not just a new version of the Lotus Sutra but a new version of religion itself, it is sure to face unique challenges over the next century. Going first entails certain responsibilities. Being in the lead means you are likely to confront certain obstacles before others even know they are there.

Predictably, the biggest challenge concerns religion itself, so much in need of an overhaul as we move into the next millennium that it is questionable whether it is any *specific* religion that needs to be reformed or reimagined so much as the whole notion of religion itself. Has humanity simply outgrown it? With racial and ethnic pluralism on the rise in nations around the world, is it not more reasonable to replace religious laws and values with their secular equivalents in order to preserve harmony and peace? These questions are now being asked in newspapers, magazines, and policy journals all across the globe.

In Western Europe we already have an answer. In nearly all of its countries—including Italy, the home of the Vatican—religion is in steep decline. The same could be said of religion in South Korea and Japan. In fact, in its most recent study of forty-four countries across the full international spectrum, the Pew Global Attitudes Project demonstrated that the higher the standard of living in a country, the less likely its citizens were to hold religious views or engage in religious activity. There were no exceptions—although the United States, at that time the most prosperous nation studied, scored highest in religiosity among developed nations. Even so, its people ranked only about half as religious as those living in poorer countries such as Indonesia or Senegal. All of which led religious scholar Alan Wolfe to conclude his *Atlantic Monthly* article on the Pew Study with words that have almost the ring of prophecy:

> The future may come sooner than we think. We have seen how rapidly religion has spread in the past, claiming adherents from competing faiths before the competition knew what hit them. Both secularism and secularly inspired ways of being religious are spreading just as rapidly—maybe even more so. Historians may one day look back on the next few decades, not as yet another era when religious conflicts enveloped countries and blew apart established societies, but as the era when secularization took over the world.

What would such a trend mean for a religious organization such as the SGI, which is poised already on the tipping point of history? The answer isn't simple.

No one can deny that until now the SGI has been a prosperity-driven movement—one that has tended to grow best and fastest among those struggling with adversity of some kind—often, although not always, economic adversity. With its teachings on self-empowerment and harnessing the power of Nam-myoho-renge-kyo to elevate one's life condition, Nichiren Buddhist teaching offers hope to people struggling in hard times. Likewise, the style of leadership and community offered by the SGI provides just the right kind of ongoing support and guidance needed to help them overcome obstacles to happiness and security. That was the pattern for the Soka Gakkai's growth in Japan and the pattern that has continued to serve the SGI as it has spread to other countries.

There is something inspiring about such a frankly populist approach. The fact that the SGI has managed to preserve that spirit of service and support to ordinary people—even years later, when so many of its members have become influential or prosperous—offers an elegant defense against those critics who saw the Soka Gakkai's early recruitment efforts as a crass attempt to exploit the nation's sick and poor. Josei Toda vowed to raise such people up—one at a time, if necessary—in order to make a stronger, healthier society. He never gave up on that mission, and the SGI continues that tradition today.

But what drives a prosperity-driven movement once prosperity has been obtained? This is a question that faces all religions moving ahead into an age of secularization—not just the SGI.

A liberal protestant minister recently told me that he had two wishes for the next decade: that church attendance would increase in the United States and that our country would succeed in legislating universal health care. I was sympathetic, but I suggested that he wasn't likely to see both wishes come true. Once a country got universal health care, attendance at religious functions invariably went down. Barack Obama had hinted as much during the 2008 election when he observed that, without adequate health insurance, all that most families had to protect them from catastrophic illness was prayer. Eliminate the threat of an uninsured medical disaster and the need for prayer was, if not exactly eliminated, then at least made far less urgent. When a state takes care of its people—*all* of its people—those people are less likely to feel that they have no choice but to take the matter before God, or perhaps chant Nam-myoho-renge-kyo.

Naturally, the SGI is not driven solely by prosperity. In recent years, under the guidance of Ikeda, the movement has become far more centered on "worldwide kosen-rufu," a term from the Lotus Sutra that means "widespread declaration of the teaching." As defined by Ikeda today, its meaning is closer to "promoting world peace through individual happiness." Nevertheless, it is important to remember that the Soka Gakkai came of age during a period of rapid postwar economic growth—a historic context that matched the optimism of the Soka Gakkai's message. If, as many economists fear, we are entering an era when economies around the world will run up against the natural limits of economic growth, that message will need to go even further in the direction of Buddhist humanism and championing the common good in order to accord with the time and the experiences of the people. Already the SGI has begun to refine its understanding of "prosperity" for an era when that experience is likely to be more modestly underwritten by prevailing economic conditions. For that transition, the Soka Gakkai's core values of peace, education, and culture—values that accord so closely with those of a modern secular state—make it a natural fit for the age ahead.

entering the age of life

A FEW YEARS AGO, I met a young Ecuadorian shaman who had been born and raised in a rainforest
region of the Amazon. He told me that in the middle of
the last century his predecessors had begun to dream
of a great catastrophe that would befall their people. At
that time they were still completely cut off from the rest
of the world. Consequently, they could not imagine what
form this coming disaster would take. Then, one day a
few years later, the bulldozers and chainsaws arrived, and
their world and their way of life began to fall apart.

This shaman told me that the elders of his people
had convened and agreed that there was no way that
they could fight such a menace. Instead, they decided
on a plan not unlike Daisaku Ikeda's strategy of kosen-
rufu through open dialogue with other cultures. Their
shamans would leave the rainforest and travel the world
with a message they hoped would benefit humanity as a
whole. They understood that a people who would destroy
the land as these invaders had done couldn't possibly
understand the balance of nature. They wouldn't stop

until they had destroyed even themselves. These rain-forest people had seen the hidden claws that Josei Toda spoke of in September 1957, and they too issued a kind of declaration: "Save us and you will also save yourself."

Much of the earth, and many, many of its species of plant and animal life, are now delivering that same message to humanity. Sadly, it is only through their disappearance that they are able to make their message known. Current estimates indicate that climate change alone could result in a catastrophic loss of biodiversity by century's end. The near-extinction of honeybees in America over the past few years is only the beginning. These species are not able to speak and conduct dialogue as the Ecuadorian shaman I met was. It falls to us to begin that dialogue, giving them the voices they need.

A Japanese Soka Gakkai member once explained to me how important it was to remember details about others' lives. President Ikeda had once told her that there was no form of compassion that rivaled this kind of "active remembering." Recalling things about another person not only let them feel known and appreciated, it actually strengthened the bond of human relationships, and that bond provided a network for positive change throughout a community, a society, even throughout the world. At the time it didn't occur to me to apply that same logic to the earth and the diversity of its species. Applied to the environment, "active remembering" becomes quite literally a lifeline to the planet, because it strengthens the bonds of life that are common to us all, providing the basis for positive change—and ultimately for a sustainable human presence on the planet.

In the end, sustainability must be the key. What is peace but a harmonious human presence on the planet? What is courage but the willingness to champion life in all its myriad forms? What is Buddhism but the opportunity to explore and celebrate our relationship with all that is, creating value rather than just money, gain that isn't based on another's loss? What is Buddhism but being awake to one's own needs and the needs of others, creating an economy of happiness that allows *everyone* to be happy?

At the beginning of my journey into the study of Japanese Buddhism, I was confused by what at first seemed a very fatalistic view of human history. Medieval Japanese Buddhists believed that the world was entering the age of decline called "The Latter Day of the Law." No longer would people be able to attain liberation through the Buddhist sutras or the practices associated with them. As a consequence human beings would become hopelessly evil, deluded, and corrupt. As if to confirm that the world had lost its spiritual balance, a series of catastrophes (not unlike the climatological disasters of today) marked Japan at the time, including earthquakes, floods, fires, famines, and epidemics that would decimate entire families, villages, and towns. Added to these were periods of social instability brought on by civil war that led even the most skeptical to conclude that the Latter Day foretold by Shakyamuni had finally arrived.

Japanese Buddhists saw the Latter Day of the Law as a guilty verdict against deluded humanity. From the vast sea of time, Shakyamuni had appeared as a savior, and for a brief period (the Former Day of the Law), deluded beings were able to attain freedom from suffering. But without the Buddha's enlightened presence to guide them, it was inevitable that they would revert to what they were before. During the Middle Day of the Law, the teachings would become overly formalized and therefore ineffective, and by the Latter Day, they wouldn't work at all.

Some of Nichiren's contemporaries put their faith in Amida Buddha, a savior who would cause them to be reborn in his heaven-like Pure Land. There, with the distractions, disasters, and defilements of the Latter Day removed, they would be able to quickly attain enlightenment. But there was no help for anyone in this world. The idea that one might turn the situation around, becoming a Buddha in this very lifetime, was almost unthinkable.

Until Nichiren.

Nichiren located Buddhahood in this body and this lifetime. There was no striving to get someplace else, no doctrine of escape from this world or its suffering, and along with that teaching came the obligation to make our peace with *this* world, not the next, and the mission to establish peace among human beings within it. As reinterpreted by Nichiren, the Latter Day of the Law became an age of kosen-rufu—a time when the teachings of the Lotus Sutra would be spread widely throughout the world.

Today, the Nichiren Buddhist teachings of the SGI have the potential to wake the Buddha, activating the enlightened potential of a struggling humanity and transforming an Age of Global Decline into an Age of Global Sustainability—an Age of Life in which one person's happiness would not be won at the expense of another's, and human progress would not be mortgaged against the degradation of the earth.

As a new model for religious faith, and for human activity in general, that reimagined Latter Day of the Law takes the long view, interpreting kosen-rufu in terms of the happiness of future generations. And those future generations of life wouldn't be limited to human generations but would include generation upon generation of plant and animal species with whom our lives are wholly interdependent. It would be an age in which the understanding of a Buddha, an Awakened One, and that of an ordinary human being were finally one in the same—an age lasting as long as ten thousand years.

That was the time frame traditionally assigned to the Latter Day of the Law. At five hundred years, the Former Day is relatively short. At one thousand, the Middle Day is scarcely longer. But the Latter Day goes on and on—its duration suggesting not so much a definite time period but rather an epoch, a period of stability in which the human presence on the planet is once more within the limits established for it by nature. An age when the Buddha and humanity itself become Awakened Ones—and the world is happy at last.

(510) 552-7920 if found

Yvonne Yamasaki